THE DAMASCUS AFFAIR

Shawn Tenbrink

ISBN: 979-8-9873592-0-4

Library of Congress Control Number: 2023930198

The views expressed in this memoir are the author's alone and do not necessarily represent those of the State Department or the U.S. government.

Cover design by Nada Orlic, erelisdesign.com
Page design by Robert Henry, righthandpublishing.com

Published by Scoutswell

First Edition, 2023

To my wife
"Love is the greatest adventure."

THE DAMASCUS AFFAIR

CHAPTER 1. Chased 1

CHAPTER 2. USA to Sham 4

CHAPTER 3. My Welcome 15

CHAPTER 4. Embassy Life 21

CHAPTER 5. Come Inside the Walls 28

CHAPTER 6. First Days 36

CHAPTER 7. Mobbed 41

CHAPTER 8. The Old City 53

CHAPTER 9. "Death Count" 58

CHAPTER 10. Official Party 62

CHAPTER 11. Social Life..66

CHAPTER 12. Relationship Challenge.................................73

CHAPTER 13. Explore 75

CHAPTER 14. Rhythm..83

CHAPTER 15. Official Party and More Mobbing...................89

CHAPTER 16. Nothing Serious 97

CHAPTER 17. Moving House 103

CHAPTER 18. The Ambassador Is Not Safe.......................109

CHAPTER 19. Halloween Party 112

CHAPTER 20. Friday Drives.......................................120

CHAPTER 21. Date Night 124

CHAPTER 22. Getting to Know 131

CHAPTER 23. Street Corners......................................135

CHAPTER 24. Listening 142

CHAPTER 25. College Party.......................................150

CHAPTER 26. GF..161

CHAPTER 27. Meet the Family 168

CHAPTER 28. Americans Need to Know 174

CHAPTER 29. Pushing Policy 184

CHAPTER 30. Breaking Down 189

CHAPTER 31. Don't Come Back 195

CHAPTER 32. Saying Goodbye....................................201

CHAPTER 33. Going Away 205

CHAPTER 34. Tragic Love..208

CHAPTER 1

Chased

STEPPING OUTSIDE, I confronted the bright Middle Eastern sun. I squinted while my eyes adjusted to the light after being inside an ancient stone church for the last ninety minutes. Standing still for a moment in a suit and tie, I saw a few people hanging out nearby in the street and a large black armored suburban in the distance.

The sleepy little town was quiet except for the bishop's voice from the church's loudspeakers. I started strolling past people sitting at cafe tables toward the black vehicle in no rush. People strolled around the town's center like it was a typical day.

Suddenly I heard something else over the bishop's voice. An old lady was yelling about something. She was angry and screaming. I mean, screaming in such a way that it made me turn around to see who needed help.

The older woman stood in the middle of the street behind me. I turned and stared at her for a second and then comprehended that she was yelling an English word over and over again: "Killer! Killer! Killer!" In my mind, I remember thinking, "That's odd for someone to scream 'killer!' in English in Syria."

I looked around to see who she was yelling at. Who was trying to kill her? My heart nearly stopped when I realized she was pointing in my direction. "Is it me? Am I the killer?"

As she pointed at me, I turned back around and briskly started walking, basically running, toward the vehicle. As I approached the car, I thought, no one knows what the new American diplomat looks like. Just because someone is yelling "killer" does not mean people are running after me.

I made it to the door of the armored car and jumped in. As I shut the door, I looked at my Syrian driver's face and saw his mouth hanging open in shock. "Shit, shit, shit," I said as I turned to look out the window in the direction I had come.

I was wrong. The older woman figured out I was the American diplomat. Getting into a giant black Suburban confirmed her suspicions. Additionally, I was wrong to think a crowd of people would not come after me.

Within seconds of entering the car, a mob surrounded the vehicle. They were not happy, cheering fans mobbing an American celebrity. No, they were an angry, screaming mob that plastered the windscreen with posters of a dictator so we couldn't drive away. Men spat on my window as they yelled curse words at me and smacked their fists on my window.

My heart rate increased as more and more people surrounded me. After entering the car, I felt safe for a second or two because I was in an up-armored Suburban. But as more and more people surrounded the vehicle, I knew if I didn't get out of there soon, I would be in big trouble.

Stuck and sweating in fear, I wondered out loud, "How the

hell did I get here?" A few weeks ago, I looked out a different window and asked myself that exact question.

CHAPTER 2
USA to Sham

MY HEAD WAS PRESSED AGAINST THE AIRPLANE WINDOW looking down at twinkling lights. At night, cities and towns look the same. Lights in the dark outlined buildings and roads, spots of darkness marked playgrounds or parks. I could be flying into Cincinnati, my hometown, but I was flying into a foreign city instead. I was flying into a job I had never done before. I was flying into Damascus, locally known as Sham. The year was 2011. The year of the Arab Spring. I was flying into a revolution.

In the seat next to me was a lovely Syrian lady with long black hair and dark eye shadow. With no in-flight movies between Istanbul and Damascus, I decided to try striking up a conversation as drinks were served. After the flight attendant handed me my drink, I turned to her and said, "Hi, I am Shawn."

"Hello, I am Rina. Nice to meet you," she responded. It was clear by her American accent that she was an American from California. As the plane traveled from Istanbul to Damascus, we both asked each other the same question, "Why in the hell are you going to Syria during an uprising, a revolution?"

Rina had just graduated from a U.S. university and was returning to what she considered to be her home. She had been raised primarily in the U.S., but her parents had returned to Syria. Her Christian Syrian-American family hailed from a small Christian town outside the city of Homs, which would become the first city to feel the violence and destruction of the Syrian civil war. She had chosen now as the time to return to Syria as others were trying to leave, heading home to be with her parents and help them through whatever came next for her family and Syria.

Even when flying to the far end of the world, into a country ruled by a brutal regime, where terrorists live and where Israel still carried out assassinations on the streets, the person sitting next to me loved sushi and had opinions about American sports and music.

After she told me her story, she asked me why I was going to Damascus. In short order, I told her I worked for the U.S. Department of State, I was a diplomat, and going to work at the U.S. Embassy in Damascus. Sheepishly, I admitted I had never been to Syria and didn't know quite what to expect. Without hesitation, she looked me in the eyes and said, "You are going to love Syria."

I hoped she was right. I hoped I would love Syria. I remember thinking that if she was anything to go by as an example of a Syrian, I was going to get on fabulously.

I was still terrified of what I was going to find in Syria. However, a year before I got on that plane, I swore an oath to defend the Constitution against all enemies, foreign and domestic. In that oath, I swore to "discharge the duties of the office." My office was that of a Foreign Service Officer, and it was my duty to go to Syria and support U.S. policies and objectives to the best of my ability. I also hoped doing my duty would be enjoyable.

It was less than two days before this plane ride that someone walked into my shared office in the U.S. Department of State in Washington, DC, and said, "You still want to go to Damascus? If so, you can go in two days as part of the political team."

Going to Damascus did not come out of the blue. I had been preparing to go to Damascus for almost a year. Still, after the Arab Spring started in Syria, a violent attack on the U.S. Embassy in July of 2011, and the evacuation of most of the U.S. Embassy personnel, I figured I would never be allowed to go. The Embassy only consisted of a few essential staff members meant to keep it up and running—the bare bones.

To this day, I am not exactly sure why I got tapped to go because there were other people in DC who were supposed to be going to Syria, all of them senior to me. I had been with the department for less than a year. All I had done up to this point was my orientation, a few months of classical Arabic training, and a class on working in a political or economic section as a reporting officer. I did not know anything. How were they going to send me, the newbie diplomat, to Syria?

The only thing I can figure is the Department didn't have many options. It seemed like the Syrian Embassy in DC was not giving out many diplomatic visas to U.S. officials. I guess I was lucky because they issued me a diplomatic visa a few months before.

I started my Syrian visa journey on flag day when I was informed that my first assignment for the State Department would be Syria. On flag day you're given a small flag in front of everyone in your orientation class. That flag indicates where you will be going for the next two years of your life on your first tour.

I am not sure why the State Department decides to tell you your assignment in front of everyone. It seems like some kind of hazing for newbies. Some people in my class pumped their fists because they were going to a place they wanted to go. Others dissolved into angry tears because their assignments were to some far-off place they had never wanted to visit, let alone live in for two years.

I mean, really. Imagine having your heart set on being assigned to Paris, a first-world country with good health care, schools, and some of the best food in the world, and then find out in front of everyone that you and your family would be going to Nouakchott, the capital of Mauritania—a place with minimal health care, limited schooling, terrorists, no stiff drinks, and limited food options.

I think the old guard, and maybe some of the new guard at the Department, views flag day as something of a State ritual for the new class of diplomats. I can imagine fifty years ago when they got their postings and drank cocktails on the lawn, toasting their good fortune and new assignments. In a way, it's nice to know these rituals still exist, and the State Department has a few of them, but I think flag day is by far one of the most notable ones for all diplomats.

As for me, I was assigned to Damascus to be part of the Economic team. I had not asked for the Damascus assignment, but I knew, because I already spoke some Arabic from my time in

Morocco as part of The Peace Corps, that I would most likely be heading to the Middle East for my first tour. Additionally, I was an economic specialist, or in State lingo, "I am an Econ Coned Officer," so to be assigned to the Economic section also made sense.

Overall, I was thrilled with my first assignment. I had never been to Syria, but I had friends in DC who had gone there to study Arabic, and they always talked highly of the culture of the old city and the kindness of everyday Syrians.

When I was handed the Syrian flag on flag day, I had no family and friends in attendance. Flag day is one of the few days you can invite your family into the State Department to watch your name get called and to watch you walk up on stage. Many of my fellow diplomats had their spouses, kids, parents, significant others, or friends there to watch them get their flag. I had decided not to have anyone attend. I think part of me was nervous, and I did not want people to witness my disappointment. Secondly, I felt like I was going to be heading off alone to wherever I was assigned, so maybe I should get the flag alone as well. In the end, I am not sure why I didn't have anyone come.

Looking back, I regret not having my parents or other members of my family see me get my flag. Not because it would have been better for me, but because I am sure my parents would have wanted to see me walk up and get the flag. Instead, after I received my flag, I called my parents to tell them the good news. "I am going to Syria!"

For the next few months of my life, I took classical Arabic classes and learned a little about my future assignment. My

Arabic classes were at the Foreign Service Institute (FSI) just outside of DC in Virginia. In the middle of my Arabic studies, a vegetable seller in Tunisia, Mohamed Bouazizi, lit himself on fire to protest his treatment by the Tunisian autocratic regime.

At the vegetable seller's funeral, crowds chanted, "Farewell, Mohamed, we will avenge you. We weep for you today. We will make those who caused your death weep." The number of people chanting after Mohamed Bouazizi's funeral grew day by day until the people of Tunisia were able to topple the autocratic regime of Zine El Abidine Ben Ali in a mere twenty-eight days. The success of the Tunisian Revolution inspired citizens in other countries, and the revolution spread throughout the Middle East and North Africa. Citizens from those nations questioned their autocratic regimes, helmed mostly by old school dictators like Mubarak in Egypt or Gaddafi in Libya.

People were asking for democratization, a voice, and a vote in their country. Before long, a single country's revolution had grown. The call was for regimes throughout the Middle East to be removed or for significant reforms.

Each day in my Arabic classes, it seemed like a new country in the Middle East started revolting. Every week our Arabic teachers from those countries would have tears in their eyes as they watched the TV in the Arabic Department's common rooms.

Some of them cried because they were so happy. Others sobbed because they feared what would come after the dictators' removal. Many cried because they were worried for family and friends who were on the ground in those countries as the revolutions took place.

They were rightfully worried. The Arab Spring was not always peaceful. There had been a general peaceful uprising in Tunisia, but there was regime violence against protestors in Egypt and a civil war starting in Libya. The Arab Spring brought instability, war, peace, democracy, brutality, and even hope to a region that had long been stagnating from rulers who had been in power for decades.

In addition, I also witnessed diplomats who were taking Arabic with me getting reassigned. Many U.S. Embassies in the Middle East reduced diplomatic staff or even closed their embassies entirely. However, my Arabic teachers kept assuring me and the other two people in Arabic classes assigned to Syria that no Arab Spring would happen in Syria. Some teachers said the Syrian government was too strong to be toppled by protesters. Others said the Syrian President was a good guy and was not like the old-school dictators in Tunisia, Libya, or Egypt, who were toppling.

They added that the ruler of the regime, Bashar al-Assad, was a reformer and a former eye doctor, not a brutal dictator who had been in power for thirty-plus years. People said Bashar al-Assad's father, Hafez al-Assad, was the old-school dictator, but he was long dead. The father, Hafez al-Assad, was the one who came to power through a coup. He was the one who had stayed in power through violence for over thirty years. Bashar al-Assad, the son who had taken over after his father's death a few years before, was different, people said. People also said that Bashar al-Assad, the son, was Western—he had a Western wife and young kids, he was a man of change, and he was a reformer, not a dictator.

Eventually, the Arab Spring did come to Syria. Adolescent

boys were tortured in the Southern Syrian city of Daraa after spray-painting a few walls with words like, "Freedom. Down with the regime. Your turn Doctor." This was the test to see who Bashar al-Assad really was. Would he be the reformer people had told me he was, or would he be the autocratic dictator of a regime?

Members of the Syrian public demanded the boys' release and for their torturers to face justice. No justice came. Average Syrians started to raise their voices asking for reforms. The call for reforms materialized through peaceful marches in many Syrian cities. By the time I had finished Arabic classes, the rallies had become protests. The Syrian Arab Spring was in full swing, and there was an uprising in Syria.

The U.S. was not content sitting on the sidelines as things heated up. The Syrian Regime was angry with the U.S. Ambassador to Syria, Robert Ford, who went to the Syrian city of Hama in support of the protestors. After the U.S. Ambassador visited Hama, the U.S. Embassy was violently attacked by pro-government thugs who blamed the Arab Spring protests on the U.S.

The Embassy sent home all the diplomats' family members. In addition, the majority of the U.S. Embassy staff left the country. In State Department lingo, it was an "ordered departure," which means American Embassy personnel are ordered to leave. In addition, diplomats who were supposed to be going to Syria, including me, were told they would be reassigned.

However, bureaucracy meant my reassignment did not go quickly. I think the process was so slow because many people at the State Department and throughout the world thought things in Syria might calm down if Assad started meaningful reforms.

Because I had no new assignment, the Department told me to apply for a Syrian diplomatic visa. A few weeks later, the Syrian Embassy in Washington issued my diplomatic visa, which shocked me as I knew other people had applied before me but never had theirs issued. I was happy to have it in my diplomatic passport, even though I doubted I would ever get to use it.

By the time my Arabic classes ended, Syria had not calmed down, and it seemed more and more likely I would be going to Syria. I was detailed on a month-to-month basis to the Syria team in Washington, known in State lingo as the Syrian Desk, until they figured out what to do with me.

Being delayed from going abroad was just fine with my girl-friend Alice. We had started dating while I was in Arabic class, but we'd known each other since our days in Peace Corps Morocco. I was attracted to her from the day I met her in Morocco. She had long curly hair, a full sleeve of tattoos, and a beautiful smile. She was also an adventurous woman who had spent the last year backpacking around Africa. She had just gotten back to the U.S. a few months earlier, and we had hit it off while she was passing through DC en route to her family in Chicago. Our relationship progressed quickly because I asked her if she wanted to move in with me in DC instead of moving back into her parent's home in Chicago. To my shock she agreed, and suddenly we were living with each other in the basement of a shared house with three other housemates in Capitol Hill.

It was an oddly bohemian existence in that house that seemed to continue my Peace Corps and Grad school days. The place was nice, but it was not really furnished. Our lack of furniture made room for our constant parties that filled up the space. The only bad part about our arrangement was the lack of privacy. It only offered Alice and me privacy when I pulled down an old grade school map in front of our bed that shielded us from the view of the stairs and the washing machines which everyone in the house used.

I enjoyed those months living with Alice, even if we had little to no money and lived in a basement room. We were happy. However, the relationship had its issues. Paramount among them was both of us knowing from the beginning of our relationship that I would be leaving.

At first, leaving for Syria seemed fine because Alice could easily come and visit me there. Before the Arab Spring, it would not have been difficult for American tourists to travel to Damascus. But with the start of the revolution in Syria, it became clear that she would not be coming to visit me if I went. I think she was hoping I would be reassigned to another country, but she never said that to me.

A few weeks after I started working at the Syria desk, a senior diplomat working on Syria walked into my tiny shared office space. I thought he would be handing me more paperwork requiring me to run up and down the halls or make phone calls like a good bureaucrat.

That day I thought, "Great, more paper." Instead, he looked at me and said, "Do you want to go to Syria as a political officer?" I was in shock and honestly thought it was a joke, but his face made me reconsider. He was serious. So, instead of laughing out loud, I managed to stammer, "Sure." His response was, "Great!"

I was not thinking of Alice when I said, "great." I wanted to leave DC and head off on the adventure I'd spent months getting ready for. I was excited that I would be going, but I dreaded breaking the news to Alice.

There was no easy way to tell her the news, so when I got home, I told her very directly that I would be leaving in two days. At first, I think she was a little shocked and said, "Really?" She had been watching the news about Syria. As I shook my head yes, her eyes welled up with tears, and she walked over and embraced me.

The following two days, I was busy trying to get everything ready to depart, and Alice was getting ready to move into her own place. Those two days were not happy days for either of us. We spent a lot of time in silence because neither of us wanted to ask the big question. Was this the end of us?

Eventually, we had the conversation. We tried to discuss our future together. We thought maybe, somehow, we could make it work, that we would stay together. I mean, there was a good chance I would be back in DC in a few weeks. Syria was a mess. Maybe they would close the Embassy in a week or two and I would return to DC. Neither of us had any idea what our future would hold.

The day I left DC, we had both said, "I love you." It was the first time we had said those words, but I am not sure I meant true love. Some languages have different words to express different levels or types of love. The love I felt for my girlfriend was not everlasting. It was a different type of love. I cared about her, but I was choosing to leave her.

CHAPTER 3
My Welcome

THE PLANE LANDED ON AUGUST 11, 2011. I got up from my seat and said goodbye to Rina. She promised to friend me on Facebook and meet me someday in Damascus to show me a good sushi restaurant.

As I touched down in Damascus and entered the 1970s designed Damascus International Airport, it did not feel like I was entering a country going through a revolution, uprising, or civil war. Instead, it just felt like I had entered a 1970s time capsule. Things felt very typical because when a country is burning, it's not all on fire at the same time. People were at the airport meeting relatives and giving each other hugs with smiles on their faces. Tired passengers were getting off of planes and rushing to relieve themselves at the nearest bathroom.

In some odd way, I think I expected to get off the plane in a war zone. I pictured myself rushing off the plane directly into a motorcade and being whisked away to a secure compound. From the news stations in the U.S., it seemed like all of Syria was in turmoil, but things felt relaxed as I walked through the airport.

Arabic signs dotted the arrivals hall. I knew I was in a country with some security concerns because soldiers walked around with the most famous Russian gun in history, the AK-47. However, seeing AK-47s is not too shocking, since even a stroll through Grand Central Station in New York City will afford you views of U.S. soldiers with AR-15s.

The most stressful thing about arriving in Damascus was the fact that I had no working cell phone. I always think about the bygone times of the telegram or when people had to send letters that read, "I am taking passage on the Trafalgar Steamer, and we should arrive in the next two weeks. I hope to see you at the dock." Without a working cell phone, I was just hoping the Embassy would have someone there to meet me like we had arranged via email a few days earlier. If no one appeared to collect me, I figured I could jump into a taxi and tell the driver to take me to the U.S. Embassy.

I wandered toward the exit door after customs, dragging my two bags, and kept thinking to myself, "I hope someone is here to pick me up because I don't know this city."

Luckily for me, someone met me at the airport. It was the person I would be replacing, Kareem Botros. Kareem was a first-generation American whose parents had migrated to the U.S. from Egypt. He had studied to be a lawyer but had joined the State Department instead of practicing law, a seemingly common career switch for former lawyers who hated their previous profession. He was also on his first tour and had been in Syria for a little over a year. He had been there with his wife, but she had left a few months before when things first took a turn for the worse.

When I came out of customs, I did not know who Kareem was or what he looked like, so I started scanning the faces in the crowd and the signs held by drivers, hoping I would see a familiar face or a sign with my name on it. I saw neither of those two things as I walked out, so I continued walking toward the crowd of people waiting for their loved ones.

As I came close to the crowd of people, one person stepped out of the mix. Kareem was not in the formal State Department business suit when he welcomed me. He had on casual, after-work clothes, and he looked like he was going to settle into his couch at home after getting me squared away.

I wondered for a second if this was indeed the person I should be meeting, but as he stuck out his hand and said, "Welcome to Damascus," I could hear a lovely, clear American accent. Behind the smile he flashed to me when we shook hands, I could see that he was tired. I wondered if one day I would also have a tired look on my face. I thanked him for meeting me at the airport as we left in an Embassy-provided black suburban and headed toward my new apartment.

As we drove from the airport into Damascus, I looked out the window, and instead of twinkling lights from a thousand feet above, I could now clearly see the streetlights and apartment windows of what looked to be a modern city. Damascus has been inhabited since 8,000 or 10,000 BC, but as we pulled into the neighborhood of Kafar Sousah, the city did not look or feel old.

This area of town was where all the new development was taking place, and it did not have the old charm of other Arab cities I've visited. There were no narrow, winding streets. My neighborhood did not look like a walking part of the city. Each apartment building had parking lots on the first floor, and the streets looked wide, but the sidewalks were narrow. The sidewalk had trees planted in them, but the trees were so young they had little shade to offer people, only providing enough to the wandering cats.

After stopping outside of what Kareem told me was my apartment building, we walked together through a fancy lobby to the elevators. As we entered the building, the first thing I thought was, "This building is nice. I have made it. I am a diplomat."

In comparison to my abode in Washington, DC, this apartment felt luxurious. I had been renting the basement room of a Capitol Hill rowhouse for four hundred dollars a month before arriving in Damascus. My DC room was one ample space that included the washing machines, which my three other housemates used. I could see the house pipes running along the ceiling, and in some spots, I had to duck to avoid hitting my head. When the toilet flushed above me, I could hear it down in the basement.

Now I suddenly felt rich as I stepped across the threshold of the apartment door. I was immediately taken aback by the style of the place and its size. In the Middle East, most people don't move out of their family home until they have their own family. Apartments there are not for single people or even a couple. They are for large families.

Not only was my new apartment large, but it was also lovely. The apartment was modern, air-conditioned, heated, and clean. It seemed like no one had ever lived there before me. The place had a new car smell and felt more like a hotel suite than my new apartment. The State Department had fully furnished it as well.

The furnishings the State Department uses are nearly identical all over the world. It comes from the same company in the U.S., and the Department ships this furniture worldwide.

Now, the furniture was not to my taste, as it was all a little too fancy. Everything was dark wood, and the couches looked like they were for cocktail parties, not for lounging on to watch college football. I had a large china cabinet in the living room. "Who the hell still shows off their china," I thought as I walked from room to room. Of course, some diplomats still do, which is sad, but true.

I had arrived on a Thursday, but it felt like a Friday night in the U.S. because the weekend in Damascus, as in most of the Arab world, is on Friday and Saturday. I would have had the next two days to get over my jet lag and settle into my new apartment in normal times, but August 2011 was not typical. Since the beginning of the uprising, the Embassy was not working on a regular schedule. The political section was working every Friday for sure and most likely every Saturday as well. Kareem told me he would be back to collect me the following day and drive me to the Embassy. "Get some rest," he said, laughing before he walked to the front door and let himself out.

After Kareem left, I looked around my new apartment and thought, "Man, I can throw one hell of a party in this place. But first things first, which bedroom do I want to move into?" Walking through all the rooms again, I quickly identified the master bedroom by its private balcony and a huge attached bathroom. Additionally, it had closets that lined the walls with floor-to-ceiling mirrors. Whoever designed this place thought the occu-pant would have at least fifty pairs of shoes and enough suits to wear a different one each day of the month. I emptied my two suitcases into those massive closets and found out it filled about four percent of the space.

Before going to bed, I walked out on my bedroom balcony. It had a plastic table and chairs, and I sat down in one, letting out a deep sigh. It had been a stressful few days, but I had finally ar-rived in Syria. I found myself looking out over the streets around my place. I could see a little bit of a park down the road and a few other apartment buildings with shops. I thought that it would be fun to explore this area, this city, and this country. There was so much I wanted to do, but at the same time, I was jet-lagged and needed some sleep.

A lot had happened in the last few days. I had moved across the world, left my girlfriend but hadn't broken up with her. I had no working cell phone and no internet. I had no friends in my new city. I had not even been able to call or email people in the U.S. to tell them I had arrived safely. Lying in my new bed, I was lonely. I think this feeling is why most people never move far away from home and why most people who do move far away from home only do it once; they realize how lonely you are when you're far from home.

Even though I was lonely, I was also excited. In many ways, the life inside of an embassy was still a vast unknown for me. The following day, I would finally get to rip open the packaging and see the inner workings of the U.S. Embassy in Syria.

CHAPTER **4**

Embassy Life

DIPLOMATS START THEIR DAYS LIKE EVERYONE ELSE. They get out of bed, longing for more sleep. After they get up, they usually shower before wandering slowly to the kitchen for coffee.

On my first morning in Damascus, I was in desperate need of coffee because I had a bad case of jet lag. In my new apartment, there was a single pack of instant coffee that Kareem had left. The Nescafe was not great, but it gave me the pep I needed. As I sat in my kitchen drinking my coffee, I wondered how Alice was doing in DC. Last night was the first time I had slept alone for a long time, and I missed having her next to me.

However, I shrugged off those lonely feelings as I finished my coffee and headed to my bedroom to suit up. On my first day, I put on a blue, one-hundred-and-fifty-dollar suit from Men's Warehouse, a white shirt, and a red tie..Before joining the Department, I had never even owned a new suit. I had purchased my suits for high school dances or other functions at Goodwill. Those used suits never fit right, but when they only cost four dollars, what did I really have to complain about? After joining the Department, I bought one gray suit, one black suit, and one blue suit. I arrived in Damascus with all three of them. I felt like I was about ready to be a diplomat as I suited up to meet Kareem outside of my house at eight that morning.

I remember looking at myself in my suit as I stood in front of my wall of mirrors, thinking to myself, "I look and feel like a diplomat, but I still don't understand what it means to represent the United States of America."

I took the elevator down to the first floor and walked outside into the Middle Eastern sun. Kareem was waiting for me in a black Volkswagen Jetta. He motioned to me, and I hopped in. The minute my ass hit the seat, he started to tell me about my new neighborhood, pointing out different shops and restaurants on the drive. As he talked, I frantically tried to memorize the route he took from my apartment to the U.S. Embassy.

Although the two-mile route from my apartment to the Embassy had a few twists and turns, it was relatively easy to remember. However, there was one big obstacle I would face on my daily route to work: the Umayyad Square, or—as I liked to call it—Damascus roulette. This square is a giant roundabout with lanes of traffic flowing in and out from seven of the city's most important, biggest, and busiest streets and highways.

From watching Kareem navigate the square, it was all about timing when you entered the fast merry-go-round of cars, trucks, and motorbikes all going at least thirty miles per hour. The use of horns seemed encouraged, and the speed limits were merely a suggestion. The streets were full of beautiful chaos as cars and motorbikes beeped their way around buses and trucks, ignoring the white lines and speed limits some engineers had hoped years earlier would somehow tame the street. I wondered if I would ever experience driving in the chaos.

Important Syrian government buildings line the square, including the Ministry of Defense, headquarters for the Syrian Armed Forces, and the Syrian National Opera House. In the center of the large roundabout is a large Sword Monument to remind the Syrian people of their victories, strengths, and achievements. This square was also the spot in August 2011 where the famous Syrian cartoonist, Ali Farzat, was grabbed by masked gunmen believed to be part of the security forces and a pro-government militia. The men assaulted him, focusing mainly on his hands to try and make sure he did not draw any more cartoons criticizing the Assad Regime. So, I guess I'm lucky I never got in an accident or was grabbed from the square since I would pass through it every day on my way to work.

I did not own a car and had no idea how to go about buying one in Damascus. Before leaving the U.S., I had read up on the State Department's briefing material on Syria, which indicated that it might be a good idea to have some wheels when living in Damascus. With its small alleys and walking areas, Old Damascus only makes up a small percentage of the city. Most modern-day Damascus is designed like U.S. cities. The automobile is king, and everything revolves around the almighty car.

Even though I thought I would need a car to get around Damascus, I didn't want to spend a lot of money on a car that I might have to leave behind. I figured I would be the guy always bumming rides from others or would make friends with Syrian taxi drivers.

However, on the drive, Kareem said, "Do you want to buy this car? It is a good car, and I need to get rid of it. I will give you a good price."

"Let me think about it and get back to you by the end of the day," I responded, but I knew I would be buying it, because how often does a car just fall into your lap?

War is overwhelmingly destructive, but sometimes there are opportunities. For example, when it comes to people trying to sell things quickly before they flee the country, there are some great opportunities to buy things at a steep discount.

By the end of the day, I agreed to buy Kareem's black stick shift Jetta at a price well below the Kelley Blue Book value—it was sold to me at a price at which if I needed to leave it at the Damascus airport as I bordered the last plane out of the country I could live with.

But I wasn't thinking about the car when we pulled in front of the U.S. Embassy for the first time. Many people might have a picture in their minds of what an embassy should look like. I find most people think embassies look like one of two things: either a fortress with high walls, or an old French chateau-looking mansion.

Embassy Damascus was a cross between fortress, mansion, and county jail. As I arrived at the front door of the complex, it looked impressive, with a nice sign indicating I was at the U.S. Embassy and big, bulletproof windows which were reminiscent of prison glass.

Cement and metal fences topped with razor wire lined the compound's perimeter. Behind the walls, I saw the outline of an old mansion that once had windows and balconies. However, now the windows and balconies were filled in with cement blocks and thick, milky bulletproof glass. The estate had become a big, ugly white lockbox.

The windows and the U.S. Embassy sign at the main entrance were still damaged by the mob that attacked the Embassy the month before, July 11, 2011. The attack happened after four busloads of regime supporters had been dropped off next to the Embassy and engaged in what Secretary of State Hillary Clinton called an "orchestrated attack" on the Embassy. Within minutes of arriving, these "demonstrators" had climbed our high walls and made it over the razor wire fences with military-style skills, smashed the outside security windows, and successfully climbed the roof of the Embassy and removed the U.S. flag.

The *Washington Post* wrote that the attack, "Highlighted the vulnerability of American diplomats in the Syrian capital." I agree the attack did highlight the vulnerabilities of the Embassy; it is crucial to understand that any embassy, anywhere in the world, is only as secure as the host nation makes it. That means the Embassy was only secure if the Syrian government, the Assad Regime, helped protect it with its security forces.

Many films portray U.S. Embassies with dozens of U.S. Marines on top of the wall. Well, in 2011, that was not the case in Damascus. The United States had around a dozen Marine Security Guards (MSGs) and a few members of Diplomatic Security (DS)there to protect the Embassy. We also had a small local guard force, but these local Syrian guards were not armed.

After the first attack on the Embassy, I had hoped that the U.S.

government would have sent in dozens of Marines and more DS agents to help. Obviously, after the attack, we needed a lot more people with guns to guard the walls.

However, there was no way the U.S. government could bring in more armed security to protect the Embassy. The regime would have never issued them visas. No helicopter was going to swoop in with a detachment of Marines to secure the Embassy. The Syrian government was holding the Embassy hostage. We all knew the regime could send over another mob. They could let terrorists out of jails to attack us with car bombs—God knows they had them there. They could have sent students to storm the place, and we could have another Iranian hostage-taking situation. The Assad Regime's security forces were our protectors, and they were also our attackers. What a lovely spot to be stuck in.

The calculation at the time of my arrival was that the Assad Regime had not yet reached the point of wanting to take Americans hostage or kill us. If they wanted to do either of those things, they could have.

In the July 2011 attack on the U.S. Embassy, it was the Assad Regime who attacked the Embassy. So, on one hand, the regime was saying, "We will protect your Embassy with our security forces," and on the other hand, they were sending those same security force members to attack it.

One interesting note on the July 2011 attack is that the Assad Regime agreed to pay for the damages to the Embassy. It was their fault for not protecting us from the mob that the regime had organized. I got to see the spreadsheet we sent the Syrian Regime listing the costs for the damages. It went into the hundreds of thousands, but the last line on the spreadsheet was the cost of the American Flag the mob had taken. The price listed was "priceless." In the end, the flag was returned to the Embassy by the Assad Regime, so I guess they did not have the funds to cover "priceless."

Everyone at the Embassy understood that U.S. diplomats in Syria were not safe. People at the Embassy understood the danger but believed the risks were worth taking and we should remain in Syria and keep the Embassy open. Maybe the MSGs didn't have a choice, but everyone else, for the most part, had the option to leave if they wanted. That was why Kareem was leaving.

CHAPTER 5

Come Inside the Walls

ON MY FIRST DAY, I had not yet realized we were neither secure nor safe. The neighborhood looked nice and calm. The Embassy walls looked big, and I could not have climbed them. We were safe, or so I thought as Kareem parked his car on a side street near the Embassy.

As we were parking, Kareem pointed out some of the Syrian security members standing around. Some were in plain clothes while others had on Syrian military or police uniforms. When Kareem and I got out of the car, a Syrian security member on the street near us waved and said, "Hi."

It's strange that the people who attack you are also the people who say hi. However, I believe that violence is not always personal, and hatred between countries does not have to exist as hatred between people. It makes sense to me that the Syrian security member would say hi to us, but, if ordered, would not have hesitated to hurt me.

The side street was a short walk away from the employee entrance at the Embassy. After entering through a security door at the Embassy, Kareem took me to the old mansion on the compound, which had transformed over the years into the main building at the Embassy we call the chancery. Inside, some people worked in old bedrooms, some in living rooms, and some in old sunrooms which no longer let any light in. The place was cut up, split apart, and walled off over the years, resulting in a hideous interior.

Kareem walked me into one of the rooms—an old bedroom filled with desks arranged to maximize the small space. He told me to choose a desk. I got to pick because most of the desks were empty. All the empty desks gave the place a ghostly vibe. I chose a desk close to a frosted security window on the side of the building facing the street. Then Kareem took me to meet my new boss, Laura Clayton, who everyone just called Clayton.

Before that moment, I'd had little to no communication with Clayton. We had emailed a few times, and people in Washington who knew her told me she was brilliant. I like intelligent people, so I thought we would get along well.

Clayton was around forty years old with dark brown hair down below her shoulders, intense dark eyes, smiley cheeks, and, I would later learn, a powerful yelling voice. From our first interaction, I could tell she was intelligent; she spoke multiple languages and had a quick wit. I could also tell she was overworked, stressed, and a little frustrated by the whole situation.

She put on a good face and greeted me warmly but quickly moved off formalities and started to explain what she expected from me. Clayton made it clear that work was going to be overwhelming and all-encompassing. Specifically, she said I would oversee the daily cable, the sitrep, for Embassy Damascus.

Sitrep is short for "situational report" and is a State Department cable—a written report typed up and emailed back to Washington, DC. The length and topic of the sitrep cable can differ from day to day, but the purpose of the sitrep is to keep the U.S. government informed about the local situation in Syria.

When Clayton told me the sitrep would be my number one priority, all I could think was, "I've never really written even one official cable." Honestly, I had only written one practice cable during a class in Washington that was supposed to teach me the basics of being a political or economic officer. Just one practice cable!

I guess, unlike other first-tour political or economic officers, I would not get trained slowly over months by my boss before I got to release my first cable. I would not get months or weeks to become familiar with my job. I was tossed into the deep end.

In my head, I was already responding with an extended version of the word "shit," but when Clayton told me I would be doing the daily sitrep, my external response was to smile and say, "Great!"

The rest of the day passed by in a blur. After talking to Clayton, I went around the office and met my new American colleagues. I lost track of the names and positions of the few Americans who remained in the Embassy. I was also taken out of the chancery to another building and introduced to the Syrians who worked at the Embassy.

State Department HR labeled the Syrians working at the Embassy as Locally Engaged Staff (LES). The term to describe the locals who work at U.S. Embassies always seems to be changing. No one has quite figured out the best term or acronym to describe these great people who are critical to any U.S. Embassy. I just called them friends or colleagues instead of whatever term HR used.

In Syria, I worked closely with two locals. By the time I arrived in August, one of them had been beaten by regime thugs. His ribs were broken, and I could still see bruises when I met him that first time. Instead of running away after the attack, he still came into the office every day, helping the U.S. understand Syria and helping push U.S. foreign policy.

I said earlier the regime had not yet decided to hurt us. I should correct that to say the regime was not harming Americans. They seemed to have no problem hurting their fellow Syrians who were working for us and with us.

Syria had dozens of intelligence and security services and agencies tasked with various jobs, but they all shared one main goal—to keep the regime in power. The regime's intelligence and security apparatus was one of the strongest in the Middle East. In Syria, they ruled supreme.

The regime was everywhere and nowhere at the same time. You never knew if a Syrian was a member of a security agency. Or maybe they weren't a member, but just an informant.

Syrians told me stories of how brothers would work for different services and agencies but not know the other one did too. I even heard stories of one security agency arresting somebody from another security agency because they did not know who was working for whom.

Oddly, the checks and balances in Syria consisted of the different services and agencies going after one another. With each one distrusting the other, the system kept itself in check by ensuring no single service or agency consolidated all the power.

The regime's strategy of having everyone suspicious of everyone else kept them in power. If you were Syrian, you might suspect friends, family members, or neighbors as being part of one of the agencies and services. You would always be worried about crossing a line by saying or doing the wrong thing in front of an informer. You would only know you did something wrong when someone knocked on your door late at night.

You could feel the regime's strength all around you because the mystery remained: who was working with them or for them? The Assad Regime used this mystery to their advantage. For example, let's say an opposition activist makes his name known at protests because he always speaks publicly. Yet, he isn't arrested. Syrians might say, "Well, he actually must be part of the agencies or services because he was not arrested." The Assad Regime could easily discredit someone, not by flipping them or sending them to a secret prison, but by simply doing nothing.

The most feared security apparatus was the Syrian Air Force Intelligence Directorate. This group was the most powerful because the former ruler of Syria, Hafez al-Assad, was a commander in the Syrian Air Force before going into politics by staging a coup d'etat. Under Hafez's Presidency, he built this group into the most robust, most capable, and most feared security agency in Syria. Syrians told me, "If you are taken by one of the other agencies, there is hope you will return, but when the Air Force Intelligence takes you, there is no hope."

But on my first day when I met with Ambassador Ford, I was not fully aware of the brutality of the Syrian security agencies and the willingness of the regime to use them. I found that out later. Instead, when I met the Ambassador, a man in his fifties with glasses and a slight build, we did not dwell on the negatives. He told me there was still hope for reforms to come to Syria instead of a civil war. As he talked to me that day, I became inspired by his words. I came away from our meeting thinking he genuinely cared about Syria. I believed he wanted real and meaningful reforms which would help Syrians, the international community, and the United States. Everyone would win with these reforms, but Syria would lose if there was violence and war.

That first week I had another reminder of the danger that surrounded me when a member of the Diplomatic Security team walked into my new office and offered me some advice. "You should take the desk across the hall," he said.

I looked at him with a blank face. I thought to myself, "What is he talking about?"

He must've seen my confusion because he clarified, "If a bomb goes off in the street there, you will for sure be dead in this office. Maybe switch to the other side of the hall. There are open desks across there."

It is not every day someone tells you to switch desks, so you don't die in a bombing. I decided to follow his advice and told him, "Great to meet you. You are right. I will switch desks."

He then popped his head back out of the office and walked away like nothing had happened. After he left, I quickly logged off the computer, picked up my cup, pen, and notebook, and moved across the hall to the open desk. Perhaps this sounds overly dramatic, being told to move desks because of "car bombs," but what he said had already almost happened.

On the morning of September 12, 2006, four terrorist attackers assaulted the U.S. Embassy in Damascus. During the attack, they failed to detonate a large car bomb which would have been just outside the window next to my first desk. Whoever was sitting at that desk in 2006 was very lucky because the bomb never went off.

The Embassy attack is not in the collective memory of the American people because no U.S. personnel were killed or wounded. The attackers came to the Embassy with hand grenades, assault rifles, and a car bomb. The result was three attackers killed by Syrian security personnel just outside the Embassy walls. The other terrorist was captured but died later during "questioning." Other than the terrorist attackers, a Syrian security member was killed.

After the attack, Secretary of State Condoleezza Rice praised Syrian security agents for repelling the attack. However, there have always been questions over who was really behind the attack and who supported the attackers. I cannot answer these questions. But I wondered if the same kind of attack occurred in 2011, would the Syrian security forces around the Embassy protect it, or would they let the terrorists over the walls? Either way, I moved desks.

Returning to my apartment that evening, I once again found myself alone in bed, wondering what Alice was doing in DC. If she was here, what would I tell her about my first day? Would I tell her that car bombs were now a concern of mine when choosing my work desk? Would that freak her out?

It didn't matter what I would have told her because I had no way of calling her. The Embassy had given me a local cell phone that day, but I was not supposed to use a work phone for a personal call to the U.S. I also had no internet in my apartment to Skype her. I felt cut off from her and the world I had left behind.

CHAPTER 6

First Days

FOR MY FIRST FEW DAYS IN DAMASCUS, I was lucky to have Kareem with me. These "introduction days" with Kareem made one thing very clear to me: it was going to be hard to meet with Syrians in Damascus, which is an essential part of any political officer's job.

As the new guy in Damascus in the time of the Arab Spring and the ramp-up to a violent civil war, it would be next to impossible for me to get to know people and then have them trust me with their opinions or secrets. It was also tricky because many Syrians didn't trust Americans, especially Americans who worked at the Embassy.

For their entire lives, Syrians have been told by the Assad Regime that American administrations are evil and advised not to trust them. The U.S. and Syria have been on opposite sides of politics and the battlefields of the Middle East and the world for decades. Syria is with Iran, Russia, Hizballah, etc., and the U.S. is with Saudi Arabia, Israel, the European Union, etc.—opposite sides.

Within a few days, Kareem left for the U.S. to be with his wife.

The day he left I felt very alone. I had spent almost all my waking moments with him those first few days. He had shown me around town, introduced me to a few people, and tried to give me the lay of the land. Now he was gone and I was on my own. When he left, he shook my hand and said, "Stay safe."

Meanwhile, back in DC, over the past five months of the Syrian uprising, more and more people seemed to have "Syria" added to their portfolios and areas of responsibility. When anything becomes the topic of the day in DC, as Syria was in 2011, people suddenly come out of the woodwork as "Syrian experts…"

The majority of the experts, by mid-August, had advised the U.S. administration to push for democratic reforms to occur in Syria. The administration was also vocal against the brutal crackdown by the Syrian regime on innocent protestors, as up until this point in the uprising, it was estimated that the regime had already killed around two thousand people.

Overall, the U.S. policy centered on sanctions. As Secretary of State Hillary Rodham Clinton put it, the sanctions would "strike at the heart of the regime" by depriving it of the hard currency needed to finance its security forces. Even with increased sanctions rolling out against the regime, it was clear the violence was not abating. Still, many people in DC thought Assad would be gone in a matter of weeks—they believed Assad would choose to step aside and leave Syria by taking asylum somewhere in a friendly nation.

Like the rest of the world, Washington had no idea if Assad was going to leave but hoped he would leave peacefully and quickly. Somehow "experts" became obsessed with the concept of "the silent majority." The idea that most Syrians were opposed to the regime but were remaining silent due to fear of the regime. The experts believed something needed to be done to inspire the "silent majority."

On Thursday, August 18, during my first full week in the Embassy, as the day came to an end, the news ticker started to carry a story that caused me and everyone else in the office to shake their heads in disbelief. The headline read, "Obama called on Assad to Resign."

Had we all missed the note from DC? The notice would have said, "We are making a huge policy shift." I thought we were still merely asking Assad to reform, but instead Obama came out and said, "Its people must determine the future of Syria, but President Bashar al-Assad is standing in their way." Obama went on to say, "We have consistently said that President Assad must lead a democratic transition or get out of the way. He has not led. For the sake of the Syrian people, the time has come for President Assad to step down."

In addition to telling Assad to step down, Obama announced another round of U.S. sanctions. The sanctions were substantial, but the shift of U.S. policy on Assad was the big news. News articles quickly started to come out about how members of the Obama administration decided to shift in policy since Turkish negotiations had stalled with Assad. Additionally, it seemed like the U.S. was not the only one changing the policy. France, Germany, and the UK all joined Obama and put out their statements calling on Assad "to face the reality of the complete rejection of his regime by the Syrian people and to step aside."

Minutes after Obama's statement, the phones in the office started ringing. Reporters from all the major outlets and papers were ringing up every phone in the section. They all wanted a quote about what Obama had just done. I remember picking up one of the calls and getting questioned, responding politely with "no comment," and hanging up the phone. After one call, I decided not to answer the phone again for some time, but they kept on ringing and ringing.

A few minutes after the announcement, members of Diplomatic Security (DS) showed up in the political section with red, angry faces. "Did you know about this?" they demanded. "Why were we not told?" This kind of U.S. statement from the President is the kind of thing that gets buses of protestors to show up outside the Embassy.

We had to tell the DS guys that we also knew nothing. Zero. We had no idea this was coming. It seemed like the U.S. administration had done a great job coordinating with foreign countries like the UK, France, and Germany, but they had forgotten to tell their people in Syria.

The DS agents shook their heads when they started realizing, like we all did, that DC sometimes cared more about headlines than they cared about people. With that, the DS agents told everyone to stop what they were doing and go home. If Obama's statement did draw a response from the regime, the fewer people at the Embassy, the better. We all turned off our computers, grabbed our jackets, and walked quickly out of the Embassy.

To this day, I still wonder where in the DC bureaucracy the Embassy was forgotten. I spent the rest of that day near my apartment going to local shops to buy a few odds and ends. I kept waiting for my cell phone to ring to inform me there were buses of people coming to the Embassy. In the end, I never got that call, and I am thankful that Obama's statement did not elicit a violent reaction from Assad.

The statement did, however, ratchet tensions to the next level. Syria's U.N. Ambassador Bashar al-Jaafari's response summed up Syria's reaction to Obama's policy shift. He said that the United States was "launching a humanitarian and diplomatic war." However, I would remove most of the words in that sentence to get to the heart of the matter. What Jaafari was saying was: "WAR."

After I read Jaafari's statement I thought, "I might not be in Damascus much longer if Syria thinks we're declaring war on them. Maybe it will be a matter of days until the Syrian government kicks us out? I am sure Alice would be happy to have me back in DC after just spending a week apart."

I talked to her that first week from a cafe with WiFi. She had asked me then, "How long do you think you will be there?" "I am not sure," was all I could answer. She kept on trying to pull information from me. She wanted to know what life and work was like for me in Damascus, but I brushed off her questions. I responded with simple quick answers: "It's interesting," "it's okay," "it's nice." I could hear the frustration in her voice when I didn't open up. I was blocking her out of my new life abroad because I did not want to share my fears. Our conversation that day at the cafe was brief and unfulfilling for both of us.

CHAPTER 7

Mobbed

DURING MY SECOND WEEK ON THE JOB at Embassy Damascus, I got a taste of what Ambassador Ford meant by getting out there and meeting people. It was a Friday, a weekend day in Syria, but since we worked at least six days a week, I was in the Embassy pulling together the sitrep.

Friday sitreps were usually more interesting than the other days of the week because Friday was "protest day." It was a protest day because Syrians had the day off of work and because Friday was the day practicing Muslims would head to the mosques. Crowds gathered at the mosques or elsewhere and protests happened, which meant extra information to put into the sitrep.

That Friday, the big difference was that Ambassador Ford walked into my office a few minutes after I completed the sitrep. He asked me, "What are you going to do the rest of the day?"

He was not asking this question to be friendly or to pass the time. I could tell by the tone that what he meant was, "I have something I want you to do."

So I told him, "I have nothing going on," and with that, he launched into what he wanted. It seemed that Ambassador Ford had been invited to a ceremony at the Church of Saint George in the ancient Christian town of Maaloula later that Friday.

I had never heard of Maaloula. Later I discovered that it is one of the only places in the world where locals still speak Western Neo-Aramaic—the same language Jesus most likely spoke thousands of years ago. Maaloula is also a popular summer spot for Syrians from Damascus because the town is located in the much cooler mountains. Maaloula is also known for its large monasteries and churches, such as the Saint Sarkis Monastic Complex and the Convent of Saint Thecla. Tragically, the town would later be known in the Syrian Civil War as the place where the terrorist group Al-Nusra Front killed many people and took twelve orthodox nuns hostage.

At the time, I understood that the Ambassador wanted me to go to some town outside of Damascus. It would be the first time I got to represent the Embassy and the first time I got to leave the Damascus city limits.

I told Ambassador Ford that I would be happy to go. With that, he looked at me and said, "Thanks. If I go, there will be a problem, but if you go, it should be okay."

When he said those words to me, their importance did not register at the time. What Ford was referring to was the fact that, at this point in the Syrian uprising, Ambassador Ford had become a celebrity for people who were demanding reform in Syria.

Ford had become a celebrity because, back in July 2011, he had visited the city of Hama. According to the *New York Times*,

Hama was a focal point early in the uprising against President Bashar al-Assad. The State Department's spokeswoman, Victoria Nuland, said Ford traveled to Hama as a show of solidarity with the residents and "spent the day expressing... deep support for the right of the Syrian people to assemble peacefully and to express themselves."

That show of solidarity got so much press in and outside of Syria that the Assad Regime did not want to let that happen again. The opposition to the regime saw Ford as one of their biggest supporters and thus saw the United States as a supporter of their causes as well.

Ford suspected that if he went to Maaloula there was a chance another commotion would occur. Ford had to pick his public appearances carefully. I think he didn't want to trigger additional restrictions and harassment from the regime.

Ford's trip to Hama prompted the regime's rule that U.S. diplomats could not travel more than fifty kilometers from Damascus without asking for approval. Luckily for me, Maaloula was only fifty-six kilometers away, a short distance more than the approved fifty, which might go unnoticed. More importantly, Ford's trip to Hama incited the mob attack on the Embassy compound back in July. It made sense that Ford should not go, so I agreed to go and called Embassy motor pool to get a car and driver to take me to the service.

An hour later I was being driven north from Damascus toward Maaloula in a nice big black American armored Suburban. The driver was a pleasant Syrian local and we had an enjoyable chat as we drove through the rocky hills outside of Damascus.

The landscape reminded me of the Anti-Atlas Mountains of Morocco that I had lived in for two years during my time in the Peace Corps. It was beautiful to be out of the city and in surroundings that seemed somewhat familiar to me. Eventually, we pulled into Maaloula, but neither my driver nor I had any idea where in town the church event would take place. I could see a few different churches popping up from the small town's skyline, so instead of driving around we stopped in the town's center.

I stepped out of the car and saw a procession of people heading toward a large church and figured I would follow them. My driver said he would wait for me in the town's center as I followed people I hoped were going to the same event that I was supposed to attend.

I walked with the group of people into a large stone cathedral. The building looked ancient. Inside, I looked around and thought about the thousands of years this place had stood in this spot. In some ways, this church felt familiar to me as I had attended both Catholic grade school and high school and thus had spent a lot of time in churches over the years.

Just after entering the church, I was stopped by a middle-aged Syrian man. I am sure he stopped me because I was the random Westerner who had entered the church, and I am also sure I looked a little lost.

As he approached me, I figured he was more than just some attendee. He had on a nice suit and looked somewhat "church official." I asked if I could sit in the back of the church and he said yes, but also asked me where I was from.

I could have lied and said I was from Canada if I had thought

I was in danger by making it known I was American. However, walking into the ancient building, everything felt peaceful and calm.

Also, on this day, I was there as a diplomat and thus could not just say the United States. So, I said to the man, "I am here representing the U.S. Embassy."

When he heard that, I could tell that he wasn't going to let me sit in the back of the Church. Instead, he looked at me and said, "Let me take you to your seat."

He led me past row after row of church pews. I suddenly realized that he was not just giving me an okay seat, he was sitting me in the front pew of the church. There goes blending in and observing; I would now be the one being observed.

Before sitting down, I shook hands with the people seated next to me. In the process of shaking hands, I was a little shocked to discover that I was seated next to the French Ambassador. This was the same French Ambassador that our Ambassador Ford went with to Hama. The same French Ambassador that the Assad Regime did not like.

Shortly after taking my place in the front row, the ceremony kicked off. It felt similar to the Catholic masses I grew up attending until the bishop, who was leading the ceremony, decided to welcome everyone seated in the front row.

He welcomed us by addressing us from his place at the altar. The bishop sounded like someone who had perfected a booming, deep vocal cadence learned through years spent preaching to crowds of people.

Despite the bishop's booming voice, his words were amplified out of loudspeakers to the crowds in the church and to the people outside of the church. I think the whole town of Maaloula could probably hear him speaking.

He moved down the first row saying everyone's name and thanking them for coming. I could tell he knew everyone in that first row until he got to me. When he got to me, he looked kind of confused as to why this young guy was in the first row, the VIP seats. Everyone else up there with me was at least ten-plus years my senior.

He quickly got over his confusion and asked me in Arabic, "Who are you?"

I replied, "I am here representing the U.S. Embassy." Again, this was not a time I could have said, "I am Canadian."

His confused state changed and he smiled at me as he said in perfect English, "Make sure America knows to be more flexible."

With that comment, some people in the crowded church, the ones I'm guessing who understood English, had a little laugh. I nodded to him to make sure he knew I also understood what he said. It was clear to me that he did not support the U.S.'s Syrian policy.

After I nodded, he moved on to the French Ambassador, who the bishop addressed in French. I am not sure what he said to the French Ambassador since I only had a crude understanding of French at the time, but the bishop said more words to him than he said to me. Also, the tone of the bishop's voice sounded like he was scolding a child for doing something wrong. All I know for sure is that the bishop was not heaping praise onto the French Ambassador.

The crowded church sat there in silence listening to what I think was a scolding. It seemed crazy to me that the bishop would invite French and American officials to this ceremony for the explicit purpose of having the opportunity to berate them and their national policies in front of an audience. "Getting yelled at for U.S. policies and actions is just part of the job" I thought as I continued sitting there, unaware that I should be worried.

After that, the bishop moved on and introduced a few more people before he turned back to continue with the ceremony. A few minutes later, the French Ambassador rose from the pew and shook the hands of people seated near him, including me. He said to me, simply, that he had to leave.

As he started to walk away from the front row, many other people seated behind him rose to go with him. His security detail I guessed. I noticed that they did not leave via the main door in the rear of the church. Instead, they slipped quietly out of the side door. Nothing in the exit of the French Ambassador gave me any need to worry. "He is a busy guy," I thought. "I'm sure he has other events to attend on a Friday night. It makes sense that he's leaving before the ceremony is finished."

The ceremony dragged on, not missing a beat even during the exit of the French Ambassador. I started checking my watch and figured that I might also have to leave early because I needed to be back in Damascus before nightfall. Additionally, my brain was tired from trying to decipher Arabic from the pulpit.

Like the French Ambassador, I stood and shook the hands of the people around me and said my quiet goodbyes as the Bishop continued with the ceremony. Unlike the French Ambassador, I started walking toward the main door of the church, the same door I had entered through.

When I exited the church, that's when I heard the word "killer" screamed at me and a mob started chasing after me as I ran toward my car.

My driver and I had not said a word to each other since I had entered the car. We both just sat there staring at the mob. Eventually, the driver started to cover his face so that people in the mob with cell phone cameras could not take his picture.

I was trying to figure out what options I had. I figured I could demand that the driver lay on the horn and hit the gas. However, with the number of people in the mob, I am sure we would have run people over. That would most likely have made the mob even angrier, and I did not want to suffer mob justice.

Instead, I sat there in the car with the driver in silence. People continued to surround us, yell at us, and spit on the car, but no one seemed to be hitting the car, which I felt good about. But after a minute or two, as the mob got more fired up, a few people started to rock the car and bang on the hood and doors. It seemed like the longer we stayed there doing nothing, the more the crowd grew.

Maybe I should have told the driver to hit the gas right away. I think if the mob had started smashing the windows, I would have told the driver to hit the gas, but thank God that didn't happen.

A Syrian policeman stepped into view and started yelling at the mob of people in front of the car. The posters of Assad were removed from the front windshield and the police officer motioned for us to drive. My driver did not need to be told a second time—we shot out of the small hole in the mob the lone officer had cleared.

Within a few speedy seconds we were exiting the town of Maaloula and everything felt normal again. It was shocking how quickly I went from an extreme moment of fear to one of peace. We were out of danger.

The driver and I stayed silent for a few more minutes as we drove out of town. Then the driver let out a big sigh. We shared a look and both started laughing. I am not sure why we laughed, but it felt great.

After the laughter ended, he told me that at some point after I had entered the church, people had come up to him and asked who he had dropped off. He did not say an American diplomat, but a rich Lebanese Christian businessman, which is one of the few people in that part of the world who might also be rolling in a big black Suburban.

The driver noticed people starting to gather outside of the church after the loudspeakers announced, via the bishop's booming voice, that an American diplomat and the French Ambassador were inside. The driver had wanted to call me, to warn me, but he didn't know my cell phone number. Rather, he sat there and waited for me. That was the last time I left an Embassy driver without giving him my cell number. The very last time.

I then called the Embassy to tell them what had happened and we were instructed to head directly back to the Embassy. We got back around dusk and I debriefed with the Diplomatic Security guys for a bit to tell them the whole story.

I finally got to leave the Embassy, and I returned to my large, golden-mirrored apartment. After getting home and showering, I felt like I needed some alone time to decompress from the day.

I walked out onto my bedroom balcony with a full glass of whiskey and a pack of cigarettes.

It had been about a year since I had regularly smoked cigarettes. Unlike most people, I had never tried cigarettes as a teenager. I had my first cigarette when I was twenty-two years old in Morocco. In the Middle East, smoking was a way to culturally integrate with other men, as sitting around cafes and smoking seemed to be part of so many men's daily routines.

My first cigarette when I arrived in Damascus was with Laura Clayton standing outside of the chancery. The best time to have a conversation with her was while having a cigarette, so I bought a pack early that week so I didn't have to keep bumming hers. That was the pack I now brought outside with me that night to calm my nerves.

My peaceful late-night drinking and smoking festival by myself on the balcony did not stay peaceful and quiet. That Friday night, August 26, was also "Laylat al-Qadr," or the Night of Power.

The Night of Power is the night when the Prophet Mohammad received the first verses of the Koran. As part of the Night of Power, many Muslims spend the entire night praying in their local mosques. Down the street from my apartment, people were praying at the Abdul Karim al-Rifai Mosque, but they also were making speeches against the regime.

Sitting on my balcony, slightly intoxicated, I did not hear people yelling in the mosque or security forces pounding on the door. Instead, the first thing that got my attention was the sound of gunfire.

As the shots rang out in the otherwise quiet Damascus night, I sat there listening. Finally, it registered. "Are those gunshots?" I asked myself. "Should I go inside?"

Instead of doing the logical thing and going inside an inner room to protect myself against gunfire, I just turned off my balcony's light. I sat there in the darkness, sipping my drink and taking long drags on my cigarette. The only way anyone would know I was up there was by the slight, red glow of my cigarette while I smoked.

Shortly after the sounds of the shots, I saw people below me on the street running away from the mosque. They were chased by a few members of the security forces. At that moment, one of the Diplomatic Security guys called me and said, "We have reports of a shooting near your apartment." I responded with, "Yep, I am watching it happen right now." There was a pause, and then he said, "Be safe and stay inside."

After that conversation, I filled up another glass of Black Label, lit up another cigarette, and continued to watch people scurry below me in the dark.

I did not see anyone get shot that night, and I did not see the security forces catch any of the people they were chasing, but I only had a narrow view of the streets and the area near the mosque.

Things on the streets settled down after thirty minutes, but I continued to sit on the balcony listening to the silence return to the Damascus night. Sitting in the quiet, I thought about how, in a few weeks, my life had dramatically changed. I was no longer safe at home with Alice. I had left the safety and comfort of the

U.S. behind. I was surrounded by the anger, instability, and fear of Syria. I thought out loud, "Will being mobbed and hearing gunshots become normal to me?"

I wished I had someone to talk to that night. Someone that could understand. But I had no friends in Damascus that I could talk to. I was not going to call my boss Clayton late at night to tell her my feelings. I could not call Alice because I don't think she would have understood. I was there on that balcony by myself. Just me and my thoughts.

I walked inside and got into bed, alone.

CHAPTER 8

The Old City

THE SATURDAY MORNING AFTER MY EVENTFUL FRIDAY, I decided to
see Damascus's old city. I brushed off my low from the night before. It was my first actual day off since I arrived. I was not going
to let the events of Friday stop me from having fun.

I was particularly excited about seeing the ancient city because I was a history major. I'd much rather see historical sites
than almost anything else when I have free time. I felt lucky to be
in Damascus, a city of history founded in the third millennium
B.C., making it the oldest continually inhabited capital in the
world, a place where cafes are older than the United States of
America.

That Saturday morning, I jumped into a taxi and directed the
driver to take me to the walled part of ancient Damascus, a
UNESCO World Heritage Site. I did not have a Syrian driving
license, so I still took taxis despite my newly purchased Jetta in
my apartment's parking lot. Even if I would have been allowed
to drive, I was happy taking a taxi since I didn't yet know my
way around the city. Specifically, I told the taxi driver to drop me

at Bab Sharqi, the eastern gate, also known as the Gate of the Sun.

This gate is one of the eight ancient gates of the walled part of the city. The gate was built by the Romans and is still standing to this day—how cool is that? It is also the gate that brings you directly into the Christian quarter of the old city.

Walking into the old city, I was transported back in time. I was now on streets that are too small for most cars, in small alleys whose doors open into courtyards of old palaces and storehouses.

I wished I could enter each one, but the doors were shut because families and businesses were working and living in them. The old city is not abandoned. It is not an archaeological site. It is a city that continues to function like it has for thousands of years. Kids still play in the alleys. Small stores, cafes, and restaurants are still open for business.

I walked down Straight Street, which is referenced in the Bible as the place where Saint Paul was converted, and bought a coffee. Next, I visited the house of Saint Ananias, a disciple of Jesus who baptized Saint Paul mentioned in the Acts of the Apostles, with its small underground chapel.

It was such a grand old city that, before the uprising, the ancient city of Damascus was becoming a destination for Western tourists because of its beauty and charm. However, when I was there, the tourists had vanished, and the stores hawking goods to foreigners were empty. Nevertheless, there were still plenty of stores and places catering to locals, so the old city was far from dead.

At midday that Saturday, the old cobblestone streets and alleys weren't overly crowded, and the sun was shining. The air smelled old as I strolled around looking at ancient buildings and breathing in the air of history.

As I was trying to lose myself in the old city, I heard someone saying in English, "Hello, please stop. Hold on a minute." For a split second, I thought to myself, "Is this another mobbing?"

Instead, walking toward me was a slender thirty-year-old Western-looking and well-dressed man. He said, "Hello," and introduced himself as someone who worked at the French Embassy. "Nice to meet you," I replied. Then he asked me, "Are you the American that was in Maaloula yesterday?" This question struck me as very, very odd, but I responded with a stammered, "Ye-es."

With that, the man flashed a huge grin. I could tell that, in a way, he was proud of himself for recognizing me. He then said, "Oh, did you get out okay? I am sorry we kind of left you there."

At this point, I realized two things: One, he must have been one of the people who left with the French Ambassador. How else would he have recognized me and known I was there? Two, it seemed as if the French must have left because they knew trouble was brewing outside. However, they had left without giving me a heads up that I should leave. With that realization, I smiled at him and said, "You should have told me it was time to go."

He laughed. "Well, next time we will," he said and handed me his business card. I thought, "Okay, well, I guess in Damascus, this is how you get to meet people." I told him I didn't have a business card myself as they were still being printed. With that, he once again said he was happy I got out okay and we both continued on our separate paths through the old city. As I walked away, I thought to myself, "That was an odd encounter, and why didn't the French tell me to leave?"

My trek that day was not my last walk through the old city. On the contrary, that area of Damascus became my favorite place to wander when I was free. Walking around the old city allowed me to be transported to a different time. A time when there was no uprising, no revolution, no social media, no sitreps. A place where it felt like there was a better chance of a medieval siege than protests.

If the old city has a heart, it is the giant mosque in the center, which I loved visiting the most. The Umayyad Mosque, or the Great Mosque of Damascus, is one of the loveliest buildings I've ever had the honor of entering. The history of the building is in its thousands of stones cut thousands of years ago.

It was first a thundergod temple before the Romans made it a temple to Jupiter. Then it was a Christian Basilica to Saint John the Baptist, reportedly still interred there, and then it became a mosque when the Muslims conquered the city. But, regardless of what religion calls this place theirs, the architecture says that it belongs to everyone.

The ceiling in the central area is over a hundred feet high, held up by the most enormous cedar beams I have ever seen. Even the beams holding up the roof most likely predate Jesus.

The stone walls are from the Romans. The stone columns are also Roman. The giant dome looks Christian, and the over two-hundred-feet high tower of the minaret comes from the Muslims. This building is history through the ages, rulers, religions, and people who have called this ancient city home.

Entering the mosque, I took off my shoes, walked into the building, and sat in the coolness of the large room, relaxing on the carpets that covered the ground. I would also walk around the courtyard on stones that were so smooth it felt like walking on ice on a lake.

I visited the gardens next to the mosque where the great Muslim warrior sultan Saladin is entombed. The same Saladin fought the crusaders and won back Jerusalem and Palestine for his kingdom that stretched from Egypt to Syria.

Being in that building gave me hope for Syria. Syria has gone through so many battles, revolutions, wars, famines, feasts, struggles, and more over thousands of years, but that building still stands. "If this building can still stand, change through time, and grow, then so can present-day Syria," I thought.

After exploring the old city for hours, the sky started changing to the bright orange of dusk, and the mosques started their calls to prayer. The sounds from dozens of mosques in the old city echoed through the small streets.

My feelings that night as I got lost in the old city were different from the night before. Instead of anger, I felt happiness. Instead of instability, I felt longevity. Instead of fear, I felt hope. But I was still walking alone. I had no one there with me to share this experience. I wondered if Alice would enjoy the city as much as I was at that moment.

CHAPTER 9

"Death Count"

DURING MY FIRST WEEKS ON THE JOB, I started to form some type of routine. I was getting to the office early every day to start the sitrep. At my desk, the first thing I did was figure out how many people were killed the day before—an impossible task.

There was no way to know how many people were killed in Syria daily. So, instead, I would approximate a number that denoted that at least this many were killed. I will not explicitly explain how I compiled the "death numbers," but I can say that I looked at different sources, including pictures and videos of people being killed or of dead bodies.

I reported in the sitreps on the number of dead, and those dead had names, but those names were not crucial for my purposes; it was about trying to see if the number of deaths every day was going up or down. Was the Assad Regime still ordering live fire on protestors? Were people being rolled up by security forces on the street and returned home dead to their parents because they fell down the stairs at the prison? The big question was, which way were things heading? The "death count" was an indicator for that question.

I came to know over time that Friday's weekly protests around the country meant more deaths every Friday compared to other days of the week. In August 2011, each Friday would have a theme or a slogan created by the Local Coordination Committees (LCC) for the opposition. These themes included the Friday of "God is with us," "We Won't Kneel Except to God," "Beginnings of Victory," and "Patience and Steadfastness." These themes and slogans helped inspire thousands of people to protest every Friday, and the regime made sure some of them died in the process.

I came to know what an anti-aircraft gun looks like when it shoots at people. After that, I learned about the different ways the Assad Regime tortures people. I learned about stabbing and beating people to death, about hangings, and about ways to get rid of bodies.

During my whole time in Syria, there was only one day that I could recall that the "death count" was zero. I remember being so happy that I did not have to report any deaths. I even got up and walked around the office, telling people the good news. "Top of the morning to you. No deaths yesterday," I might have said with a smile to my colleagues.

I still think about how messed up those mornings were, trying to get the "death count." Those mornings affected me for a few years after leaving Syria. Even though I was not physically there with the bodies, I was there with them every morning at my desk.

After I figured out the death count, I would look through other information and add it to the sitrep. Usually, just before

lunch, I would send the sitrep up the chain to be cleared. As part
of that clearance, it went to my boss, Clayton. I dreaded sending
it to her because there would be a scream that I could hear from
down the hallway. Then, after the exclamation, I would be called
into her office to be yelled at for grammatical errors.

It might come as a surprise to you as you read this to learn
that I have severe dyslexia. Dyslexia doesn't mean that I cannot
write. It just means that there will be mistakes and Clayton was
the grammar police that gave me a ticket and lecture every day.
She would yell out, "What the fuck is this?!" and "Don't you
check your work?!" Getting yelled at every day after dealing
with the emotional pain of looking at dead bodies did not make
happy mornings.

In the end, Clayton would correct my grammar and move the
sitrep forward to be cleared by others, including the Ambassador. Eventually, it was sent out from the Embassy to the rest of
the U.S. government.

I know that our Embassy Damascus sitreps not only went to
the regular crowd in DC, but they also made it up the chain of
command. I know this because the information from our sitrep
was mentioned at White House press briefings. Going from not
knowing how to write a cable to having my cables referenced by
the White House would suggest I figured out how to write pretty
good sitreps, even with grammatical errors.

The sitreps might have had some impact on DC policy, but I
know they impacted me. I started to feel very removed from
things in the United States. I no longer worried about how Ohio
State football was doing. I did not care about Alice's job at a vet's

office. I lost all interest in trivial matters. They were nothing compared to the life-and-death struggle occurring in Syria.

I no longer wanted to call and talk to anyone in the U.S.—family, friends, or even Alice. None of them would understand, and I did not expect them to understand. I would talk to Clayton about Syria during smoke breaks we took together. Still, those conversations were never fulfilling. They never offered me much hope for Syria.

When I had the time after work, I would head to the old city. I walked around the narrow laneways and looked at the layers of history. I would look at all the marks on the city walls from when they had been attacked centuries ago. I would try to tell myself that, just like those past conflicts, this violence would pass.

CHAPTER 10

Official Party

I WROTE HOME TO FRIENDS AND FAMILY toward the end of August and said that I worked six days a week, but I worked on all seven days. I told friends and family via email that I was happy to be in Syria and that things were good.

Looking back, I wrote those words to make sure people at home were not worrying about me. I sugar-coated the truth or left things out entirely. I talked about my lovely apartment or told people I had bought a car. Those emails and calls with my friends and family were vague, worthless, and meaningless. The only purpose they really served was letting them know I was still alive and still in Syria.

Every time I talked to Alice during those first few weeks, she would try to get me to talk but I would remain silent. I am sure she really wanted to yell at me because I was pushing her away. Our calls and my emails kept getting shorter. It was not like she was losing me to another woman or that I was going out every night with new friends. I had no one in Syria. The only thing she was losing me to was Syria.

As I got lost in the world of revolutionary Syria, I was invited to my first semi-official Embassy party. The party was at the apartment of a military officer stationed at the Embassy for the Department of Defense (DoD).

The party guests consisted of two groups, U.S. Embassy personnel, and many military contacts, military attachés, and others from various embassies in Damascus. We all walked around this very nice apartment, sipping cocktails and eating finger food. All the military men had on their dress uniforms, and all the diplomats had on their "official" suits and ties.

In many ways, the beginning of this party felt like something you would see out of the movies. It was the picture of diplomatic life. People were having small talk while servers carried around appetizers and glasses of wine. Sometimes someone would laugh loud enough for the room to hear, and after that, it would go back to the lower levels of chatter. Men sat on the roof or on one of the balconies smoking cigars or cigarettes.

The only thing that made it un-movie-like was the fact that there were few women in attendance. In other postings worldwide, there are plenty of women in the military, or military men who bring their wives to these parties. However, the spouses of almost all of the officers from the Damascus Embassies were gone. On that night, I remember that the only women there were personnel from the U.S. Embassy.

The lack of spouses to advise their significant other not to drink or smoke too much, I think, led to higher levels of intoxication than might typically occur. Additionally, everyone with kids had sent them out of Syria, so there was no need to wake up early with the kids the next day.

Everyone at the party was knocking them back and smoking it up. I had a feeling that this party was going to go late into the evening, but instead, there was somehow a magical signal for people to start leaving after the waiters finished serving the finger food.

The foreign military men in their uniforms made their way to the door and went off into the night. All U.S. diplomats and military men stuck around to see them off, which is required when you attend a U.S. party.

As the last guests left, the party moved on and into debauchery. All of the Americans stayed, and now we didn't have to worry about what we said or who we were talking to. The business of diplomacy was over. Now it was the business of having a good time.

We had all been working long and arduous hours, and this would be the first time I got to see everyone kick back after working hours had ended. The military uniforms slowly became less formal, and State people took off their ties. The quiet chatter between people turned into drunken banter. No one had to be official any longer, and no one had to be politically correct.

The unofficial part of the night is a bit of a blur in my mind. I remember it was fun to let loose—to be free from work and forget about it for at least a few hours. Some of my colleagues danced on the roof. One of the military guys stripped down and jumped into the tiny baby pool on the roof. People started spilling drinks as they got glassy-eyed from having way too many cocktails. I spent the rest of the party on the roof, drinking with a lit cigarette in hand.

My colleagues were great. They were friendly, pleasant, and intelligent, but I never clicked with any of them for some reason. Maybe it was because I was younger than most of them. Perhaps it was because I was not married with kids like many of them were.

While being driven home by one of the members of the DS team, I remember being happy that I got to watch and hear the shenanigans of my colleagues letting loose. More importantly, it was nice to see the true personalities of people I worked with compared to their work personalities. I might have thought that the people I worked with were uptight, always put together, and disciplined, but like most people, after a few too many drinks, they became your average person that's a little rough around the edges.

The night started as a diplomatic high-class thriller movie and ended in *Animal House*. I finished my night alone again at home.

CHAPTER 11

Social Life

THAT FIRST HOUSE PARTY I ATTENDED made me feel like a one-per-center. I'd never participated in social events in the U.S. with finger food served by waiters. I figured out that a diplomat in the developing world, making a Western salary, is wealthy compared to most locals.

Being rich in Damascus meant I could not only afford lunch at the Four Seasons in Damascus. More importantly, I could afford Western goods, food, and drinks at grocery stores. I could eat at Western restaurants and have drinks at non-dive bars.

Compared to my time as a Peace Corps Volunteer in Morocco, I thought the life of a diplomat was great. I only went to Pizza Hut once in Morocco, and while there, the people sitting at a table next to mine had pizza leftovers. There was no way I was letting that good American pizza go to waste, so I ate it.

In addition to the Western restaurants, there were also high-end, delicious Syrian restaurants. Some of them used to cater to the foreign tourists in the old city. Others were old places that had been feeding the Syrian population on the cheap for decades.

When I went out to eat at expensive Western and Syrian-style establishments, they were not full of people. It seemed that the high-end restaurants of Damascus were not popular in 2011. This was mainly because the Syrian economy in 2011 was not on the up and up. The country had found itself in an economic crisis.

Before the uprising, the Atlantic Council had described Syria as a country with macroeconomic indicators that were "relatively sound" in the decade before the rebellion. After the uprising started, the Atlantic Council stated that the Syrian economy started to "deteriorate significantly." By "significantly," I think they meant to say that the Syrian pound was in free fall, prices of goods were going up, and Syrians were losing their jobs.

However, in August 2011, Syria had not reached the point of an economic collapse. Still, every day the black market exchange rate to buy U.S. dollars with Syrian pounds kept on favoring the dollars. Every day I was getting richer and richer, but what would I do with that money?

Even with bleak economic outlooks, there was one thing that younger Syrians still seemed to be okay spending money on: alcohol and partying. When things get stressful, everyone has to find a way to release or relax. For many Syrians in Damascus in 2011, that seemed to happen through a stiff drink and music.

Most people don't think of bars or clubs when they think of the Middle East, but I can tell you that from Morocco to Saudi Arabia there are party scenes fueled by alcohol. In some places, this happens underground, and in others, it's right there on the surface. This might seem strange, since most people in the Middle East and North Africa are Muslim and alcohol is forbidden. But many people in the world don't follow all the rules.

In Damascus, the bars were concentrated in two areas of the city. The first area with a lot of bars was the Christian part of the old city. Those bars never questioned someone's religion when they asked for a whiskey, wine, beer, or local arak. The second area of the city with a plethora of bars and clubs was the nice part of town. The rich people, when out, would drink expensive drinks compared to drinking at home or traveling to the Christian quarter in the old city.

There were many different types of bars in those two areas. In the Christian quarter, the bars were smaller and not as fancy. One bar there fit less than five people inside. There were also larger bars that looked similar to Irish pubs. Outside of the old city, there were clubs with bottle service that look like they were modeled after the rooftop bars in Lebanon. They would be blaring Western or Arabic music out of speakers that were taller than me. If you preferred a certain type of watering hole, you would likely be able to find something similar in Damascus and get a good stiff drink to quench your thirst.

However, I did not know any of the things I just explained. As the new guy in town, I had no idea where to go, and it was not like I could get on Yelp or some other app to find out about the hottest new place to meet people.

I had tried talking to my colleagues at the Embassy to find out where to go, but it seemed like everyone was so busy that they did not have time to hold my hand for a social night out. What seasoned diplomat wants to go drinking with a young whipper-snapper?

A few times, I had a drink with another diplomat who lived in my building. He was a great guy to bullshit with on the balcony, but we were at different stages in life. He was not looking to meet new people and hang out at bars. His wife was in the U.S., and he was happy to talk to her every night, which is understandable.

The only people at work who I thought I could maybe fit in with were the Marines. They were closer to my age and, for the most part, seemed like they were ready to go out. I thought maybe they could help me fill in the gaping hole of a social life I had for those first few weeks.

Every day walking into the Embassy, I passed at least one Marine. That Marine would be sitting behind bulletproof glass, armed and in uniform, waiting to buzz me into the chancery and my office after checking my ID.

My first impression of the Marines was that these guys were serious young men and might not jive well with me, a former Peace Corps guy. However, as I passed them day after day, I got to know their faces and names. After the first few days of entering the Embassy, I had started to stop and talk to them through the small opening in the bulletproof glass that people slid passports and ID badges through to gain entrance.

After many rounds of BS, I finally asked one of the more friendly Marines where I should go out in Damascus. Really, I was trying to get an invite from him to go out with the Marines for drinks. I knew that they would go out and usually in a group, so I figured maybe they would take me along. I did not want just to get the name of a bar and head off to drink alone.

The MSGs in Damascus represented a cross section of the U.S., from good old boys to city guys. They were a cast of characters that came in all shapes and sizes. There was a giant Marine, maybe six-foot-four. There was the ripped Marine that drank milk all day and night.

The first time I went out with the Marines was in early September. They told me to meet them for drinks at a bar that was less than a mile from the Embassy. I was excited that I was finally going to have a night out. A chance to BS with people close to my age over drinks.

The bar where I met them was called 808. The place presented itself as a cafe, but it was indeed a bar. In fact, it was a basement bar that had no genuine windows. Even the front door was made from a glass mirror that didn't let sunlight pass through it.

It was not a large bar but could easily fit fifty people if some of them stood. It had comfortable tables and a nice bar that you could sit at. It was well lit so you could see everyone—there were no dark corners. Also, it mainly played Western tunes, and the music was not too loud.

Having the music volume at the right level is really what made this bar great for me. Many times in the Middle East and elsewhere, the bars crank the music so loud all day and night that I can never have a conversation. However, 808 did have late-night dance parties, but not until very late. I believe that the owner once lived in the U.S. at some point, and he kind of made the place feel like a U.S.-style establishment.

One of the most memorable nights I had with the Marines at the bar was a few weeks after arriving in Damascus. It was a

Friday night, the best of all nights to go out and have a few too many drinks since Saturday was the most leisurely, most relaxing day of the week for me.

I got to the bar just after dark and sat down at a table with a few of the MSGs. The night progressed, and soon the drunk personalities of a few people started to appear—there was the happy drunk, the tough drunk, the ladies' man drunk, or the sad drunk.

Unfortunately for me, the Marine sitting across from me that night had transitioned into a sad drunk. He was repeatedly trying to tell me sad stories of war. I was not looking to talk through sad stories that night as I had enough tragic stories in the daily sitrep. I was already surrounded by enough violence in the office and did not want my Friday night out to be spoiled by more sadness.

Instead of facing the sad guy across from me, I turned my head and was chatting with someone farther down the table. I was laughing and talking with someone else when suddenly I felt a burning pain on my left hand. My head snapped back, and I locked eyes with the big, sad Marine sitting across from me. He now had a drunken smile on his face and gestured toward the table with his eyes. I looked down and realized why my left hand was in pain.

His hand was hovering above mine, then he slowly raised it to his mouth. Between his fingers was a lit cigarette that he calmly continued to smoke.

I lifted my arm to take a close look at my hand and it became painfully obvious he had burnt a circular hole into it. The wound was not that painful yet because all of the nerve endings had been burnt and I had a few glasses of whiskey already in me. I guess he really wanted my attention and at this point he had it. All of it.

I jumped out of my seat and started to yell at the Marine, "What the fuck! You don't do that to people! You want to talk to me, tell me! Don't fucking burn me."

The Marine's face slowly moved from the smile back to the sad face as he could see I was upset with him. He quickly stuck his hand out with the still-lit cigarette and said, "Here, just burn me back and we will be even."

I angrily replied to his offer by saying, "That is not how this works. This is not an eye for an eye thing."

I stayed mad at him the rest of the night and did not talk to him the rest of the evening. He continued to try and find ways to get my forgiveness, which included an offer to just "punch me in the face, and we will be even."

I was not going to punch or burn him to make us even. I just kept putting ice on the wound and drinking. Getting my hand burnt was not going to ruin my first night out.

When I saw the Marine a few days later before coming into the chancery, I was no longer mad. Instead, we both laughed about what had happened. I did make him promise he would no longer burn people with cigarettes at bars if they were not listening to him.

Even though I could now laugh at the burn wound, I had to spend the next few weeks trying to hide my left hand when at internal or external meetings. I was sure that if anyone saw the wound on my left hand, it would be obvious that a cigarette had been put out on it, and I did not feel like telling people what had happened. It was an embarrassment.

CHAPTER 12

Relationship Challenge

I STARTED TO RECOGNIZE OTHER PEOPLE AT THE 808 BAR after going out with the Marines over the next few weeks. Eventually, after sitting in a smoke-filled basement bar with a glass of whiskey, I generated enough liquid courage to start talking to other people in the bar.

The bar brought together a mix of expats, diplomats, and Syrians, and in a short period of time, I started to get to know some of them. Hanging out with the MSGs was a good time, but I also wanted to branch out from the Embassy. I thought it would be good for work and also for life.

Over time, one person introduced me to another person, and then another, and so on. After less than one month of going out, I had built up an okay Rolodex of acquaintances who were on their way to becoming friends.

As I was making friends in Damascus, I often thought about Alice back in DC. Was she hanging out with our friends there? Was she having a good time without me? I did not know the answers to those questions because I never asked her.

I communicated with her via email and with a few calls after arriving. However, in all those communications, I was distant, and I am sure she felt it. I should have just ended the relationship, but I was a coward.

Eventually, during a skype conversation, she brought up the idea of ending our relationship. I don't remember her exact words, but she said something along the lines of "I don't think this is working."

That could have been my opportunity to jump in and say we shouldn't end our relationship and that we could make this work. But I didn't jump in and say those words. I agreed that things were not working, and we both walked away from the relationship.

Being a diplomat and moving from place to place sounds great, like a wild adventure, but that adventure takes a toll on relationships. If diplomats do want to keep a relationship alive, then they need to go all in and get married. I think I knew when I left DC that I was not going to marry Alice. I was not willing to go all in.

The night we broke up, I sat on my balcony, looking out over what seemed to be a peaceful city. I thought about my sitrep from earlier in the day and the people who had been killed and vanished. I contemplated what would happen to Syria.

I was not thinking about Alice and how she was doing. I was thinking about how Syria was doing that night. I realized that maybe I had broken up with Alice because I was already in a new relationship with Syria.

CHAPTER 13

Explore

I WAS A LONER WHOSE LIFE WAS JUST WORK. I had not yet built myself a social group even though I had met more people. Hanging out by myself was rather dull, but things changed when I got my Syrian driver's permit and was allowed to drive my newly purchased car. If I felt lonely and had time, I would get in my car and roam.

Well, kind of free to roam. I was restricted in terms of where I could go. I couldn't leave the city of Damascus because the Syrian government did not allow it. They said it was for our safety, but I am sure that they did not want us traveling around the country to all the violent revolutionary hotspots popping up in other Syrian cities, like the city of Homs. On September 7, the Local Coordination Committees (LCC) reported that thirty-four people were killed in Homs when tanks and twenty trucks of soldiers launched a raid in the city.

In addition to the Syrian Regime's restriction on my movements, I also had rules from Diplomatic Security. DS did not want me or others from the Embassy to drive into certain city areas because of safety concerns.

I did not care if I had some restrictions because I was still free to drive miles and miles of roads around the city. I was finally exploring the city and seeing if I could remember all of the routes I had learned from taking taxis everywhere.

The first week I had my Syrian license, I would go out in my Jetta and drive and drive with no purpose. I would put some good old classic rock tunes on and joyride around the city. I am sure the guy from Syrian security or intelligence who was most likely following me on those drives would have been shaking their heads and saying, "This guy does not know where he is going." In truth, they were right.

Driving around Damascus, I started to see the layers of a grand old city. At the center of Damascus was the old city with the oldest neighborhoods behind ancient fortress walls. There were only a few roads in the old city I could drive on, and they were always slow going since they had been constructed hundreds of years before and were not made for cars.

The old walled city represented Damascus for thousands of years, but now the city had burst outside those city walls and seemed to have been built in layers. I could drive through the next ring of the circle. That ring was made in the European style in or around the 1920s when the French, and before them the Ottomans, controlled Syria. Those buildings were large and colonial. After that circle, there were the flats of six-ish-story buildings built in the 1950s and 1960s. I did not care for those buildings' architecture. Finally, there were the new neighborhoods, like where my apartment was located. This latest circle had buildings with large glass windows and large shopping malls.

During those first few drives by myself, I started not only see-ing the layers, but the city as a whole. It struck me how this was the capital of the regime. Syrian flags were everywhere, and large pictures of Assad were pasted on walls and buildings. Govern-ment offices were everywhere in the city. I could see Syrian soldiers standing guard outside of buildings.

Driving around most days, I think people would have no idea there was an uprising, a revolution occurring. I would have be-lieved that Syrians loved the regime based on the flags and posters. The monuments in the roundabout showed the strength of the regime through the decades. In 2011, driving around Damascus, it seemed like the regime was still robust.

When friends of mine, or even my parents, watched TV in the U.S. that September, they saw images of Syria in upheaval. A place with daily protests and troops shooting civilians. There is no doubt this was happening, but that did not mean the entire country was aflame. Even years later, at the height of the Syrian Civil War, I would see pictures on friends' Facebook pages of them jet-skiing on the Syrian coast and pictures of cocktails at sunset in Damascus.

A country on fire does not mean that it all burns at once. It burns slowly from place to place. In Syria, the burning started in the southern city of Dara. That is the Syrian birthplace of the rev-olution, the city where a few youths painted anti-regime graffiti on a wall. After the boys were arrested and tortured by Syrian security, their parents asked for justice from the regime. They wanted the torturers to be punished. But the regime did nothing, so people rose up and went to the street to demand justice.

Instead of justice, those who peacefully marched were met with violence, bullets, torture, and death by the regime.

By September, the fire that had started in Dara had spread north. It touched many cities, and protests were happening all over the place, including Damascus, but the next city to burn was Homs.

Rebel groups were reportedly setting up bases of operation in and around the city of Homs. There were reported clashes between armed members of the opposition from the Free Syrian Army and the Assad Regime in the neighborhoods of Dayr Baalba. Additionally, there were protests and violence in Bab al-Sebaa and Baba Amr. It seemed that every day Homs was heating up to become the first Syrian city that saw neighborhoods reduced to rubble.

The woman that sat next to me on the plane, Rina, was heading to Homs and was living just outside the city in a Christian village. When I read, heard, and watched videos of what was happening in Homs, I would wonder how Rina was doing. Sometimes I would even message her on Facebook to see if she was still alright. Her responses to my messages were all the same. It is sad what is happening, but I am fine.

In mid-September, she messaged me and told me she was coming to Damascus to get away from village life and asked me if I wanted to grab sushi. I said yes, and we chose a day and time to meet.

Sitting just outside near the Four Seasons Hotel in Damascus ordering sushi, it struck me how crazy Syria is. Here I was talking to a beautiful woman, pretending that no significant troubles were going on around us. We could have been anywhere in the world, but we were in Syria.

I was having a good time with her as we talked between sips of beer. Our conversations over dinner started like we were on a first date. What were our dislikes and likes. We laughed and giggled as the waiter brought out our sushi. She spent a long time trying to give me advice on things to do and see in Damascus.

Then, about halfway through the sushi rolls, we started really talking, not about trivial things but about Syria and the revolution. I was taken aback by how different our two opinions were on the situation in Syria. Rina did not find the regime's violent actions wrong because she believed that the opposition were radicals. In her opinion, the regime had to fight because if it collapsed, the radical elements of Islam would enter the power vacuum and take over Syria.

I would like to believe Rina's opinion was based on supporting the devil you know compared to the devil you don't know. However, no one knew who the opposition was, and no one knew who could come next after Assad. The U.S. didn't know either, but we knew that Assad had lost his legitimacy because he had innocent blood on his hands.

All I knew sitting there eating spicy salmon sushi rolls was that I was pissed at the regime. I had met members of the "opposition," and at least the people I had met peacefully protesting were not radicals. They were not crazy Sunni extremists. They were Syrians who just wanted positive change for their country. They wanted leadership that could be held accountable.

There is no excuse for the regime's violence against innocent civilians, women, and children. No one should ever torture another human being. These are truths. For me, keeping the regime devil was not an opinion.

However, it was not up to me as a diplomat, or even up to the U.S. government, to make that decision. It had to come from the Syrian people. In truth, I think the Syrian people were mixed. Some were like Rina, with the regime, while others were against it. In 2011, no one knew which side was going to win.

So as we ate, I kept my mouth shut and full of food and beer. I still found her beautiful and engaging, but we disagreed on many things. I figured it was better to remain silent and get her perspective, even if I just wanted to yell out, "Why can't we all just get along?"

After paying the bill, we said our goodbyes as I told her to be safe in Homs. As we walked away from each other, I hoped that she would remain safe regardless of which side of the revolution she supported. I did not want to see a picture of Rina in Homs when I was doing the morning death counts for the sitrep.

In those days, I met with people that were on all sides of the revolution. I also met with corrupt people, killers, and torturers, and I found out that I could talk to someone politely, enjoy the conversation, and even enjoy them, but also know that I was completely opposed to their thoughts and/or actions. I guess being a diplomat is the art of getting along with everyone. However, in September 2011, the diplomatic world was not getting along with Syria.

The international community was trying to make a difference through words of diplomacy. On September 6, UN Secretary-General Ban Ki-moon called for Assad to take "bold and decisive measures before it's too late." He stated that UN member states should unite and take "coherent measures," but it remained unclear what "measures" really meant. Would it mean sanctions, military intervention, coups?

Ambassador Ford also continued his online campaign of words against the regime. He stated that it was clear that Mr. Assad's government had no capacity for reform. He wrote that Assad was not fooling anyone by blaming terrorists and thugs for the unrest in Syria.

By September 7, the regime canceled the Arab League's Secretary-General Nabil Elaraby's scheduled visit to Damascus due to "circumstances beyond our control." Elaraby's office said the visit had been indefinitely postponed.

The UN was drafting resolutions to condemn the violence. Security Council meetings were taking place. A war of words in speeches, on social media, on drafts of papers, and through the media was raging.

While the international community was trying to figure out what actions could be taken other than words against the Assad Regime, protestors prepared to go to the streets for another Friday of protests. The opposition was not oblivious to the diplomatic confusion on what measures to take.

On Friday, September 9, the LCCs decided that their theme for protests should be "Friday of International protection." The LCC seemed to be saying to the international community, "Please take some measures that can protect us." Protect the peaceful protestors. That Friday, the day of "International Protection," the LCC reported at least fourteen people killed at those protests.

I engaged in small "protests" of my own as I drove around Damascus in the nice part of town called west Mezzeh. This area has a Syrian airbase where many peaceful protestors vanished. The area is also where a lot of Israelis assassinated many Palestinian and Hizballah figures. It is also a beautiful part of town where some Embassies are located, and there are nice houses and apartments.

Through Mezzeh, there's a large road with four lanes of traffic going each way. It was the only spot I knew in Damascus that had a functioning speed camera. So, for my little protest, I always sped up just before reaching the camera. Then I would hold one of my five fingers out the window toward the camera as I passed. You can guess which figure it was.

I hope that in some Syrian security file on me, there are photos of me speeding by showing the regime the bird. My actions were no doubt childish and stupid, but they made me feel happy for a few fleeting moments.

CHAPTER 14
Rhythm

BY MID-SEPTEMBER, MY LIFE HAD GOTTEN INTO A RHYTHM. I had a car, a basic work schedule, an apartment, and I had started to meet people. It was time for me to write home to friends and family and tell them what I was doing and seeing. At the same time, I did not want to say too much.

I wrote home to friends and family via email that, "I have seen some messed up shit," and that, "I really just hope for peace and love." I guess the Peace Corps person my mom loved was still in me when I was writing home. I ended one of my few emails home by saying, "It seems that no matter what happens it will take time. So I figure I will be here for a bit."

I think this is important to note because, before I left for Damascus, people were saying that Syria, like other Arab Spring countries, would happen quickly—a matter of weeks, not months or years.

Either the regime would reform, or the government would collapse in a quick and disorderly manner. After a few weeks in Damascus, it was clear to me that there would be no quick resolution for this revolution.

This realization led to a mental shift for me. Instead of believing that I might only be in Damascus for a matter of days or weeks, I started to feel like I would be in Damascus for a while. I regretted not shipping anything to Damascus and only bringing two suitcases. In the end, a few more creature comforts wouldn't have mattered because my life still mostly revolved around work.

My daily sitreps continued to be sent throughout September, and Clayton continued to lecture me on my grammatical mistakes. I also started going to some meetings with Clayton.

I always enjoyed going to meetings with her because she would do most of the talking and I could sit back and learn. I tried to understand how far you could push a question if it was sensitive. I learned that cigarettes and coffee are great icebreakers at a meeting. I learned that a meeting might last an hour, but you only actually talk for a few minutes. I learned the subtle art of building relationships and not jumping straight in to get your questions answered.

Standing or sitting behind Clayton at those meetings, one funny thing did occur. Time and again, while I was standing there, people we met thought I was her bodyguard and not her colleague. I figured this out because I was not offered the coffee like she was. I guess bodyguards traditionally don't get coffee when they protect people in Damascus. I had to say something, and then the contact would say, "Oh, the bodyguard wants coffee too?"

While working on the sitreps with my colleagues, Ambassador Ford was also busy writing messages, but Ford's written words went out via the Embassy's Facebook page. The use of social media by Ford in many ways made him the number one provocateur of the regime in Syria. I can also say that nearly everyone in the Embassy agreed with the words he wrote.

He always called on the regime to make "deep, genuine, and credible reforms." He called for peace while at the same time hammering home that regime violence was not acceptable.

At the same time, Ford acknowledged that the revolution did have deaths on both sides. This was highlighted in a Facebook post where he said, "No one in the international community accepts the justification from the Syrian government that those security service members' deaths justify the daily killings, beatings, extrajudicial detentions, torture and harassment of unarmed civilian protesters."

Ford was trying to destroy the regime's narrative to justify violence. The regime kept saying it was being attacked. By September, there were some armed factions of the opposition, mostly made up of former regime soldiers who had deserted and were now engaging in clashes with the regime. However, those attacks in no way justified the regime's killing and torturing of peaceful protestors.

One memorable post by Ford to counter the regime's justification read, "Some Syrian security service members have been killed. Some want the United States to acknowledge it; well, I'm the American ambassador, and I just did." Ford's Facebook posts were, I think, more effective at gaining U.S. government support than the Embassy's sitrep. In public, he was able to be the "provocateur." He was effectively pushing policy being made thousands of miles away in DC through his action in Damascus.

I believe Ford's words via Facebook were exactly what needed to be said. He was calling out the regime, and he was not holding back. At the same time, were his harsh words always cleared by Washington before he wrote them for the world to see? I don't think so. Was that a significant risk for him? Yes, I think it was. Diplomats tend to tread lightly and defer back to DC if there is any risky language they want to use. Ford did not do this, and for this reason, his actions brought him an interesting nickname in Washington; he was and maybe still is the "undiplomatic diplomat."

This undiplomatic approach trickled down to all aspects of working life at the Embassy because I was taking my leadership from the top, and, for me, Ford was the top. If Ford wrote something on Facebook, there was no problem with me saying it to people on the streets.

The U.S. Embassy took sides and was not playing nice with our host country, Syria. We were yelling via Ford's posts at the regime to stop the violence, while simultaneously saying the protestors had "courage." The U.S. narrative had created a villain—the regime, and the hero—the peaceful protestors of the opposition.

The issue with the narrative was that it was slowly taking us down a path no one wanted to go. It was taking us to civil war. There was still hope in September 2011 that the civil war was not written in stone, that something could happen to change the path of the story. There was hope that the hero could win or the villain would somehow realize their past mistakes and reform.

Living the story daily in Syria, I still hoped that civil war would not be how it all ended. If I thought that was the only outcome, it would have made my job so much harder. Working toward a civil war was not something I could or would support.

The opposition felt similarly. Exiled Syrians abroad and dissidents inside Syria started forming groups that became the Syrian National Council (SNC). This council, like others, had plans to topple the regime quickly and created an interim government to replace the regime before fresh elections.

These plans were made mostly by people sitting safely outside of Syria. After the SNC formed, the theme for protests on September 16 was "Friday of Continuing Until We Bring Down the Regime." The people that could make the SNC's plan a reality again took to the streets all around Syria. On that day, at least eighteen peaceful protestors were killed.

The SNC was not the only game in town; the opposition was not a unified front. In Syria the day after the Friday of protests, the Arab Socialist Democratic Union party, an opposition group that the regime had previously outlawed, met in Damascus. Unlike the SNC, this opposition group released a statement after the meeting that did not call for the regime's downfall but instead called for the regime to stop acts of repression and urged protestors to remain peaceful.

Now there was opposition inside and opposition outside. There were calls for peace and calls for the regime to fall. There were many Syrians with many different plans for the way the story should go. President Obama met with Turkish Prime Minister Erdoğan and agreed to "increase pressure." I am not sure what they meant by "increase the pressure." There were so many factors already at play, but only one thing was concrete: By

September 2011, at least 2,700 people had been killed. That means 2,700 people would have still been alive if the revolution had never started.

CHAPTER 15

Official Party and More Mobbing

IN SEPTEMBER, CLAYTON CAME TO ME and gave me another task. I was to organize an official U.S. Embassy event. I am sure I said something like, "For sure! I will organize a party!"

Now, I have hosted many parties in undergraduate and graduate school. These parties usually involved kegs of beer and plastic cups. The last party I hosted was in DC to say goodbye to people, and it involved a table full of beers, little Debbie snacks, and McDonald's dollar double cheeseburgers. For music, I'd hired a local bluegrass band to play in the living room. The cost of the band was one hundred dollars plus free drinks.

As Clayton was talking to me, I found myself wondering, "Do Syrians like bluegrass?" I snapped back into reality and understood that this official Embassy representational event would not be like the previous parties I'd organized.

This party was a subtle "middle finger" gesture to the regime. The regime did not particularly want us in Syria. This was evident from the steps it took to limit our movements, disrupt meetings, and overrun the Embassy. However, we were still there, and now we were going to have a party and invite other people in Damascus to celebrate with us. To toast to us still being in Syria.

Clayton decided that the best place to host this soiree was a location less than a mile from the Presidential Palace—where Assad and his family lived. So, during an uprising, I went about planning an official U.S. Embassy event down the street from the Syrian White House.

When I went to the venue, Art House Hotel, I was a little nervous that it would be out of our price range. I guessed that having the word "art" in the title meant it had to be fancy. Truth be told, it was fancy and nice, but because there were no tourists and the Syrian economy was collapsing, the hotel was happy to rent us their roof deck for a reasonable price.

With the venue secured, I now started trying to get alcohol. I learned a valuable lesson from Clayton when I brought her the list of what I wanted to buy for drinks. She looked at my list and said, "Well, I am not sure this is enough." She then told me she would find more funds so we could buy more wine. The lesson learned is this: Always overbuy when it comes to drinks. Make sure there is enough booze. If the alcohol stops at a rep event, you will lose your friends quicker than if you invaded their country. Clayton found me more rep funds, and we were going to buy enough booze. Crisis averted.

On the Thursday morning of the event, I finished the sitrep early and started getting ready. I dropped off the booze at the Art House Hotel. I made sure the DS team was good to go with security. I went home and suited up. I took a taxi to the venue and got ready for guests to arrive.

Since I was the organizer and from the host country, this event would not be a party for me. I was working. My first job of the evening was standing outside near the hotel entrance to welcome everyone as they got out of their cars.

It was good for them to see an American face and voice as they got dropped off. It also allowed me to shake everyone's hand and introduce myself. When the guests got up to the roof, where the event was being held, they were then given the official greeting by the Ambassador and others.

By the time I finished shaking hands at the hotel entrance, people on the roof were a few glasses deep in wine. When I finally did get upstairs, what greeted me was a happening and spirited event.

Picture a rooftop dimly lit up at sunset. There were great views facing downtown Damascus. Fancy, important people were chatting away while sipping their wine. Music played in the background—low enough not to interrupt conversations. As I entered the rooftop and saw this picture, I thought to myself, "Good job." I then went around doing my second job of the evening—meeting people and talking.

Business cards were exchanged, red wine was drunk, I laughed, listened, and had a good time with our guests. I would never have known a revolution was afoot if I had seen this party from the outside. However, if I listened in on conversations, I could hear the rumbling uncertainty about Syria's future. I could listen to peoples' fear of war. I could listen to sad stories. I could hear that things in Syria were getting worse.

On that Wednesday before the event, September 21, Syria had drifted further away from the international community. Turkey announced it would cut all relations and contact with Syria. It was also announced that the coming Friday would be labeled "Friday of Unification Against the Regime." At least twelve people were killed that day.

The gathering in Damascus that Thursday helped unify me into the diplomatic world of Damascus. Shaking all those hands when people arrived familiarized me with all the faces and names in the diplomatic world in Syria. I received business cards and set up meetings for weeks to come because of that event.

I was officially in Syria now. To the regime I thought, "Piss Off—I am here to stay with my colleagues at the Embassy."

After the party was over, work went back to "normal." It was not just my life that had formed some regular daily schedule. Other diplomats in Damascus had also fallen into some sort of routine during the revolution.

My colleagues were still going out to meetings throughout Damascus. The Ambassador was also going out, even though he was being tracked and watched by the regime.

As the pressure grew from the international community and as the opposition tried to coalesce around some sort of united strategy, the regime became more and more nervous about their position of power. Protests continued throughout the country, and there were daily reports from the opposition about Syrian soldiers defecting to join armed groups of the opposition.

On September 23, it was reported that the Free Officers Movement, a group of defected Syrian military officers, had joined forces with the Free Syrian Army (FSA). The main groups that would fight the long and drawn-out civil war were forming during this time. In late September, I still hoped a civil war would be avoided, but it seemed less likely by the day.

The regime kept going back time and again to the playbook it had used for decades to quash rebellion and dissent. Their number one play was violence. The regime seemed to believe that if you hit, shot, tortured, arrested, and blew people up, the problem would go away.

The next diplomat the regime decided to intimidate was the French Ambassador, Eric Chevallier. On Saturday, September 24, the French Ambassador visited the Greek Orthodox Patriarch Ignace IV in the Christian quarter of the old city, the place where I loved spending my free time when I had time off on Saturdays.

When he left the meeting with the patriarch, a "random mob" had formed to confront him. News reports claimed that the mob began chanting in support of Assad and then started to throw eggs and stones at the French Ambassador as he made his way to his car.

The French Ambassador was quoted by news outlets after the attack as saying, "The Shabiha (pro-government thugs), some of whom had metal bars in their hands, and women threw eggs and stones in my direction and in the direction of my team, and looked threateningly at us while we were returning to our cars."

There was no doubt the regime was sending messages to diplomats by attacking the French Ambassador, but diplomats had to send a message back. That message was, we are going to continue doing business as usual. We will be meeting with people.

We will represent our national interests. Your violence will not stop us.

About a week after our official event, things in Syria started to heat up even more. On September 29, the opposition reported that they had attacked regime forces in the city of Rastan. This city lies about sixteen miles north of Homs and would become one of the major strongholds of the Syrian opposition.

The attack that day was not a minor attack on the regime. According to the opposition, seventeen Syrian tanks were destroyed. Some people said that eighty regime loyalist soldiers were killed, while others said thirty-eight soldiers were injured. Regardless of the exact numbers, actual fighting had begun between the regime and armed members of the opposition.

On that day, the regime decided it was going to make things uncomfortable again for U.S. diplomats. On September 29, Ford and others from the mission visited Hassan Abdul Azim, head of the outlawed Arab Socialist Democratic Union party, in Damascus. I was sitting at my desk at the Embassy when one of the security guys popped in and said, "Did you hear about what's happening?"

Upon Ford's arrival at the office of Hassan, a mob of around one hundred regime supporters chased him and the others into Hassan's office. Ford was hit by a tomato thrown by the mob before he was able to enter the building safely.

Ambassador Ford and others barricaded the door to the office to stop the mob from entering. The members of the security team threw their bodies against the door as the mob chanted outside.

I am not sure what I would have done if I was in Ford's

situation. Would I have frozen and cried in a corner? Would I have started making weapons out of office furniture to fling at the mob? Who knows. True to Ford's style, once the door seemed secure, he sat down and had a meeting with Hassan.

While Ford and the others were trapped, people at the Embassy were trying to figure out what the hell to do. Should we all drive down there with guns blazing? The answer, of course, was no to the guns blazing idea in diplomacy.

Instead, lots of phone calls were made to regime officials, and eventually, after around thirty minutes, Ford was able to exit the office, get back into the motorcade, and return to the Embassy.

When the motorcade flew back inside the Embassy walls, a few others and I were there to greet them. No one was injured, but nerves were shaken. People got out of the cars, cigarettes were smoked, and smiles were nervous but happy to get out of there.

The cars of the Ambassador's motorcade were damaged by more than just tomatoes or other flying fruits and vegetables. I saw where metal pipes struck the vehicles. Windows were smashed, and dents were made in the large armored Suburbans. I am sure if the mob would have caught up with Ford, those metal bars would have been used on more than just the cars.

At the same time, this mob was also holding back. If the regime had directed the mob to kill, they would have acted differently. That mob was there to intimidate and, at worse, maybe injure someone. One thing we did know is that this assault on a U.S. Ambassador was not random.

Secretary of State Clinton told the press later that day, "This attempt to intimidate our diplomats through violence is wholly unjustified." She continued and said that the regime should "take every possible step to protect our diplomats." This statement was rather funny because the mob was made up of the regime's people.

The White House that day also told the press that this attack was "an ongoing campaign to intimidate and threaten diplomats attempting to bear witness to the brutality of the Assad regime." It was true that the level of intimidation against diplomats by the regime was increasing. As pressure mounted on the regime, they were lashing out by attacking two Western Ambassadors with mobs. It was clear that the regime would not sit back and let Ford and others criticize them. To stop the Ambassadors, the Regime had turned to violence, just like they had with peaceful protestors. Violence seemed to be the only answer the regime had when trying to solve their problems.

Later that day, to somehow justify the attacks, the Syrian Foreign Ministry put out a statement that read, "Recent statements from American administration officials… clearly indicate that the United States is involved in encouraging armed groups to practice violence against the Syrian Arab Army." We were being blamed for violence against the Syrian State, so that meant they could attack diplomats.

The day after the attack on our Ambassador, Syrians again went to the streets to protest the regime. That Friday was the "Friday of Victory for the Levant and Yemen," and the opposition reported that at least thirty people died. There were also reports of more clashes and soldiers defecting from the Syrian military. Violence was getting worse, and each week the sitreps got bleaker.

CHAPTER 16

Nothing Serious

EVEN AS SYRIA WENT DEEPER INTO THE REVOLUTION, I found the bright side of revolutionary social life. Through the rep party and going out with the Marines, I had started to branch out and create a social circle outside of the U.S. Embassy. Two of the people I became closest to were Sarah and Natalie, both of whom worked for the UN. Sarah was a dual U.S. and Canadian national, tall with brown hair, while Natalie was from the UK and was beautifully black with curly hair. Both of them were always fun to talk with over cocktails and cigarettes. In addition to those two, Natalie introduced me to her love interest, Vuk, who worked at the Serbian Embassy and became a very close friend of mine.

Over time, I felt like I was making the UN Assembly of friends. There was Sebastian from the German Embassy, and a few people from the Danish, Swedish, and Norwegian Embassies. Then there were two Egyptian diplomats and a bunch of people from the Canadian and UK Embassies.

The motley crew of diplomats and UN staff that I was socializing with were primarily single, in their twenties and thirties, and stressed at work. When these groups of people got together, it seemed like everyone was ready to let loose from the stress of revolution.

In addition to going to bars or restaurants, the group also had a few house parties. A member of the Austrian Embassy had the best house party during this time. He and his family lived in an old riad in the ancient city. He had a courtyard and a rooftop terrace. Drinking cocktails at his social gathering, I felt like I could have been transported back to the times of *Lawrence of Arabia*.

As my circle started to grow, there was one thing that I noticed. It did not include many Syrians. It seemed that diplomats usually became friends with other diplomats or non-locals who also lived a transient lifestyle. Like me, these "transient people" were all looking for friends because they didn't know anyone in Syria. On the other hand, Syrians already had their friend groups and were not looking to add to them.

By October, my weekend evenings consisted of meeting a group of new friends at a bar or at someone's house. Everyone would show up looking like the workweek had crushed them. However, after a few drinks, they would start smiling, and by the end of the evening, we would all be dancing around like crazy, forgetting about the world around us.

I also started flirting with some of the women in the group during weekend parties. I flirted with someone from the Danish Red Cross, a beautiful Danish woman with short blond hair. It didn't go anywhere other than a few kisses on rooftops. There were other flirts and glances with women at bars and parties. However, I was not taking numbers or going out on dates. I was not going home with any of the women. Who had time to date during a revolution?

By early October, the SNC had announced its governing structure with the hope of uniting the Syrian opposition groups. The Syrian army was now engaging in armed clashes with the FSA in and around Homs. In addition to armed clashes, there was an uptick in assassinations. One of the most prominent assassinations was that of Mashaal Tammo, a Kurdish Syrian politician, activist, and member of the SNC from the Kurdish city of Qamishli. His killing brought thousands of Kurds into the street, which led to the deaths of at least fourteen funeral-goers.

Like many things in the revolution, both sides blamed the other for the killing of Tammo. The regime said "armed terrorists" had killed him. The Kurdistan Workers Party blamed the Turkish government for the killing. I tend to believe Tammo's son, who told the press that the regime killed his father.

Even with assassinations and clashes, peaceful protests continued. The first Friday of October was called "Friday of the Syrian National Council as Our Representative." It was the same day Tammo was assassinated.

With all this going on, I was not going to have time for a relationship. Instead, I would just continue to enjoy the time with my new diplomatic social circle.

That's why, in early October, when my buddy Sebastian from the German Embassy texted me and asked if I wanted to meet up for drinks on a random weekday at 808, I said sure. Sebastian was a German Federal Police Officer in his mid-twenties who was doing a security rotation at German Embassies. In the U.S., we have

Marines, and in Germany, they have the federal police at Embassies.

Sebastian was a character. He was always loud, always happy to drink, and always just happy. As an example of his character, he showed up to his first day of work at the Federal Police with his hair in cornrows, driving a car with scantily-clad women painted on the hood. I enjoyed his extreme character, and he was a great person to go out with since he would always laugh, drink, smoke, and joke all night long. So when he asked me to come out to 808, I agreed, but I didn't know when I decided to come that he needed my help.

Walking into the smoky 808 on that random weekday evening, I thought I was just going to get drinks with Sebastian and forget about work for a few hours. After entering the bar, I spotted Sebastian sitting at a table with two Syrian ladies. "He's made some new friends," I thought as I walked toward the table. It was not unusual for him to make new friends with whoever was sitting next to him. That was part of his character.

He stood and hugged me before introducing me to the two women sitting with him. As he introduced the first lady to me, he said, "This is my date, Zara." It was at this point I realized this was a double date. He had not just met them at the bar that evening. I guessed I was there to be his wingman, and I was happy to do it.

His date, Zara, was a lovely Syrian lady with a curvy body, bright red lips, and full black hair. After shaking her hand, Sebastian introduced me to the other Syrian lady.

She had on very little makeup, a cute face with an upturned

nose, sparkly eyes, and black hair down to her back. She was not tall or short but seemed just the right size for her slim body shape. At the time, I remember only thinking she looked beautiful. We shook hands, I introduced myself as Shawn, and she told me her name was Amal.

Once introductions were over, we all sat down and ordered the first round of drinks. It was apparent after the first few seconds that both Amal and her friend spoke excellent English.

That night, 808 was mainly empty because it was a weekday. Having the place empty ended up being great because we could easily converse over Black Labels, wines, and cigarettes without other people's voices interrupting us.

Through our conversations, I found out that Amal and her friend worked at a Western Embassy together. They were both from Damascus, and both were amazingly funny, intelligent, and interesting.

After a few rounds, Sebastian and Zara started to lean toward one another. They were now talking to each other instead of the group. It was time for me to be a wingman, so I turned to Amal, and our eyes locked.

The conversation between Amal and me that night was effortless. Unlike other "dates" I'd been on in the U.S., we did not find out that we knew the same people, studied the same thing, or liked the same music or films. Instead, we just had an effortless conversation like we had been great friends for years.

As we talked, our eyes would meet, and we would smile at one another. Amal would play with her hair as I told old stories that made her laugh. I found her infatuating, mysterious, and beautiful. It had been a long time since I had smiled and laughed so much. I also found that for those hours, all the stress of work and life melted away. As our evening came to an end, I knew I wanted to see Amal again.

When I got to Syria, it was the first time I ever had business cards. So, I reached into my pocket, pulled out a business card, and gave it to Amal.

I did not realize the faux pas I was making when giving her my business card. Giving a woman a business card means one of two things: either I was not interested in her, or I was an asshole who thought his job would get him laid. In reality, I was into her, and I also was not an asshole who thought what I did for work should get me laid.

Thank God Amal did not take offense to me handing her my business card. Instead, she took my card, put her name and number on it, and handed it back to me.

Sebastian and Zara, I think, also had a good date, but by the end of the evening, I was not paying attention to either of them. My eyes and thoughts were all on Amal, but it was a weekday, so eventually our double date came to an end.

The four of us left the bar and said our goodbyes to one another. As Amal walked away, she turned one last time and flashed me a smile before heading to her car.

I grabbed a taxi and went home to my apartment, thinking about what type of text message I would send Amal. I felt like a high schooler who got the cool girl's number and wanted to ask her to the prom.

CHAPTER 17

Moving House

THE MORNING AFTER I MET AMAL, the blissful images of her from the night before and the dream of dancing with a beautiful woman some day were gone as I got back to sitrep work. The sad stories and deaths continued.

The situation in Syria week in and week out was getting worse and worse. It was not happening suddenly, but in a slow trickle that was moving in the wrong direction. First, security forces used clubs on protesters. Then they started shooting them. Now the regime was using tanks to attack its people.

Eventually, the regime's brutality would go as far as dropping barrel bombs (big metal barrels with explosives in them) or chemical weapons on civilians sheltering in their houses—causing the numbers of the dead to go from a few up to hundreds a day.

I hoped our cables were reaching the Washington decision-makers. I also wondered if our cables were getting to the right people. However, even if they were, could someone in DC stop the violence? Was there a way to peacefully deescalate the revolution? Was there a way to bring about a positive change in Syria peacefully? How could there be peace when, by October 2011, the UN reported that around 2,900 people had been killed in the revolution?

Around this time, October 11, the regime decided it needed to show people that not everyone in Syria supported the opposition. The regime still had strong support from the Alawites, a group from Assad's religious sect. Many Christians supported the regime because they feared crazy Sunnis would take over and they would be killed or banished like what had happened to Christians in Iraq. Many Sunnis still supported Assad as they, too, feared being killed or vanished by radical extremists.

To show their support, the regime brought its people to the streets. Media reported thousands of Syrians in central Damascus chanting pro-regime slogans like, "God, Syria, and Bashar." They also shouted slogans like, "America, out, out, Syria will stay free."

Syrian state-run media announced a million people had marched "supporting national independence and rejecting intervention." I did not go down to the rally since being an American diplomat at a pro-regime rally would not have been good for my health.

Instead, I watched on TV as a helicopter flew over the rally, dangling a Syrian soldier with Chinese and Russian flags to thank those two nations for vetoing a drafted revolution against the regime at the UN Security Council.

The international community, like Syria, was being divided, and many Western and Gulf nations were lining up behind the SNC with the hope that the regime would start negotiating with them or that the SNC could overcome the regime quickly.

Overall, though, countries that supported the opposition elements struggled to push the regime to the table with the opposition. The EU, like the U.S., was throwing more and more sanctions at the regime. However, opposition forces were not relying solely on sanctions to help them win. October 14 was not the "Friday of Sanctions." It was "Friday of the Free Army."

Just like the regime held a significant rally earlier in the week, the opposition now brought their people out across the nation. The only significant difference between the pro-regime rally and the opposition protests was that opposition protesters were shot and killed when they went to the streets. According to the UN, by the end of that Friday, over 3,000 people had been killed since the start of the revolution.

Even in the revolution, things moved forward in my social life. Sebastian messaged me after the double date and told me that Zara and he had a great time and would love to go on a double date again. He also pushed me to see what I thought about Amal. I figured whatever I told him would be passed back to Zara, which would then be passed back to Amal. So, I responded with something simple, "She was lovely."

In reality, I wanted to write and say she was amazing, and I wanted to see her as soon as I could. I wanted more of that blissfully easy conversation. I wanted Amal to take me away from the world around me. I wanted to be in a small bar with her, sharing drinks, laughs, smiles, and not thinking about Syria.

Maybe that's what I should have said, but I was busy and knew that trying to start a new relationship would be very problematic. Syria and my job were my priority, and I wondered if I could or should try to date during a revolution.

In addition to work, I heard that I would be moving. The tension between the regime and the opposition now meant that living a few miles away from the Embassy in the area of Kafar Sousah was not the best option for me. I was fortunate in finding a place because another U.S. diplomat was leaving, and his apartment, which was only half a mile away from the Embassy, would be vacant.

The move itself did not take long since I had few possessions. I packed up my belongings, put them in my Jetta, and switched apartments. The entire move probably took me two hours.

My new neighborhood was Al Malky, in the heart of the Embassy and regime neighborhood. Between my apartment and the U.S. Embassy was the old Presidential Palace, and men still stood in front of it in suits with machine guns under their jackets. Trees in the neighborhood had landline phones placed in their trunks so the men in suits could get a call, which I am sure would have been helpful before cell phones.

From my new apartment, I would not be able to witness protests from my balcony like I had on the "Night of Power" in my old neighborhood. This neighborhood did not have protests against the regime because it was full of affluent Syrians who would most likely not be affluent if they did not have ties to the regime. It was also full of government offices that housed various elements of the regime. It was safe but also possibly unsafe for me at the same time.

The apartment I moved into was on the upper floor of a nice

building that I think was built sometime in the 80s. It was a vast place with three bedrooms and a living room that was big enough to play Frisbee in. On the side of the apartment facing the street, there was a large balcony with good views. However, the fixtures in my new place were not as new and not as golden as they were in my old apartment. The walls were not covered in mirrors either.

The only real problem with my new place was that the apartment was too large. I had so few things that it felt empty. I felt like a squatter who had broken in. Nothing was on the walls, no carpets on the floors, and the only furniture I had was a bed, a couch, some chairs, a small TV, and a dresser or two, all issued by the State Department.

Even though my new place was creepily empty, I was happy to be there. I enjoyed the fact that just down the street from my new place were a few shops and a small mall that I could easily walk to. My new apartment also had an underground parking garage for my car, which I thought was good. But the best part about the place was the view. This apartment building stood on the slopes of Mount Qasioun, which meant it had some sweeping views of the city.

During my first night at my new place, I left and drove up to Mount Qasioun. Near the top, there are several roadside stands where you can order a hookah. After ordering a double apple hookah, I sat on a plastic chair on the mountain, watching the sun slowly go down. The mountain felt peaceful. I did not see a city in crisis as I sat there and smoked.

With me on the mountain were Syrians also looking at the view, talking about their future hopes and dreams. It was also a popular date spot for Syrians, and there were a few couples near me holding hands. I wondered if I should take Amal there at sunset, but I had second thoughts about bringing her there because of what else was also on the mountain.

The very top of the mountain is home to a Syrian military base. It is a shame that mountain tops are strategic locations, I thought to myself. Later in the civil war, artillery shelling from that base rained down on several neighborhoods of Damascus.

While I was looking at the view of the city, the diplomatic world was still trying to figure out how to stop a civil war in Syria. In October, all eyes were on the Arab League, a union of Arab-speaking African and Asian countries who promoted independence, sovereignty, and the affairs and interests of its members, including Syria.

In October, the league was trying to bring Syria and the opposition together to create some sort of road map to keep Syria out of a civil war while simultaneously carrying out democratic reforms. To this end, the Arab League was calling for a "national dialogue." The dialogue sounded nice compared to a civil war, but I don't think people thought it would actually happen.

Other countries in the region successfully brought about change through violence. For example, on October 20, 2011, Muammar Gaddafi was killed in Libya.

So on October 21, during the "Friday of the Martyrs of the Arab Deadline" protests in Syria, some opposition members shouted that Assad would suffer the same fate as Gaddafi.

CHAPTER 18

The Ambassador Is Not Safe

THE TIMING OF MY MOVE CLOSER TO THE EMBASSY was spot on because things became a little more dangerous for U.S. diplomats. On October 23, Ambassador Ford was called back to Washington, DC, in a "surprise recall." Mark Toner, a spokesman at the State Department, said that Mr. Ford was being called back to Washington from Damascus after "credible threats against his personal safety."

I am sure Ford had credible threats against him, as the mob proved. The regime was also making up false rumors about Ford. One was a rumor that his motorcade hit and killed a Syrian child. The regime was trying to make Ford out to be a supporter of terrorists and a child killer. It seemed that the regime's intimidation was now directed at Ford.

After Washington announced that Ford would be heading back to Washington, DC, I received many emails from State colleagues, friends, and family asking if I was also leaving Damascus. It was a logical question. If there were credible threats against the Ambassador, it probably meant that there were also threats against the U.S. Embassy in general. I would have thought that we were all in danger, but that was not the calculation of those in power in DC.

The State Department's spokeswoman Victoria Nuland said on October 24 that the administration planned to send Ford back to Syria once the threat had eased. I am not sure how the threat would've eased. It was not like U.S. relations with the regime were headed in the right direction. She also added that his visit back to DC would just "give him a little bit of a break" from a harrowing assignment.

When I heard that Ford was departing, many red flags started waving in my head. For sure, Ford was a target of the regime; the planned mob attack showed that. However, if he was gone, wouldn't the regime just find another target?

To answer all the emails about Ford's departure, I responded with a simple answer, "No. I am fine. Don't worry about me. No, I don't need a break."

I could not explain to my family why the Ambassador had to leave and why it was okay for me to stay. I guess generals in the army don't fight on the front lines all the time. When things get bad, they just keep the grunts in the danger zone. Maybe I was just a grunt.

Even if I was a grunt, I don't blame Ford, our general, for leaving us. I don't think he had a choice in the matter. I thought that maybe having him go back to DC to push policy on Syria in the hallways of power could be a good thing. However, that still did not take away the feeling of being a grunt stuck in the foxhole we called the U.S. Embassy in Damascus.

While it was discomforting that Ford was leaving, it also did not surprise me that the rest of us stayed. Taking risks was part of a diplomat's job. I was in Syria on my own, in the shit, and without any real protection.

I still felt like it was helpful to have diplomats remain at the Embassy. It showed the Syrian government and the Syrian people that the U.S. was not afraid of the regime—that the U.S. was with the Syrian people and we were not running away.

I also think that having diplomats on the ground helped our messaging from DC on the regime's atrocities and crimes. If we had all left, our message would have become less credible to the Syrian people. By staying in Syria, we were saying we were not afraid of the regime, and we were going to be there with the people who were suffering. We were not like the Syrian opposition figures who fled and were sitting safely in Europe. How could peaceful protesters trust a government if it wasn't also willing to risk something?

Also, for me, I had just met Amal and wanted to see her again. This is not a good reason to stay in a revolution, I know, but it was true nonetheless.

However, not everyone at the Embassy wanted to stay in Syria. At one point, I vividly remember a member of the U.S. Embassy yelling at an internal Embassy meeting, "I do not want to die in these hallways defending this place," then added, "I don't know why we are still here."

In the midst of all of these security concerns, the Embassy did not close when Ford left. We did not hide behind the walls or stop doing our jobs. Instead, the Embassy decided it was late October, and we needed a Halloween party!

CHAPTER 19

Halloween Party

I AM NOT SURE WHY THE MARINES THOUGHT IT WAS A GOOD IDEA to have a big Halloween party less than a week after the Ambassador left due to threats. Maybe with the provocative Ambassador back in DC, security was better? Perhaps it was because the Marine's Embassy bar had not been used for a big bash since I had arrived at the Embassy.

I am unsure why having a party was approved by security, but I guess, just like the one I had organized a few weeks before, this was another middle finger to the regime. Our message this time was, you might have forced our Ambassador out, but you cannot stop the American tradition of Halloween parties!

An unintended benefit of the Halloween party was that foreign governments realized we were not planning on closing the U.S. Embassy. When Ford left, diplomats started calling, and they all asked me, "Are you closing the Embassy?" I would respond, "No, we are not closing. Actually, do you want to come to a Halloween party?" They must have been writing back to their governments in Europe and elsewhere saying something like: the

U.S. does not seem to be pulling out because they are still having parties and must not be concerned with their security.

For me, though, the most exciting reason to have the party was that it allowed me to invite Amal. We had only really met one time at 808, and we had exchanged a few text messages.

Those first messages were nothing special. They were the usual kind of messages that happen after meeting someone the first time. They went something like, "It was nice to meet you at 808." She would respond, "I really enjoyed it." I would say, "We should do something soon together." She would say, "That sounds great." Then there would be a pause in the messages because I did not ask her out.

Maybe I should have said, "Do you want to meet me in the old city tomorrow night?" Arranged a romantic dinner for just the two of us in the old city. We could sit on a rooftop during the call to prayer as the sun burned the dusk sky red. We could sip cocktails and forget about the world through effortless conversation together.

But none of that happened because I did not ask her out on a date. Instead, the first time I asked to see her again was when I invited her to the Halloween party. I was excited at the chance to see her again, but I also invited her to a large social gathering instead of being one on one. It was not a date. It was an invite to a party.

In addition to inviting Amal, I also sent invites to the UN friends and the other diplomats I had met and befriended. Almost everyone said they would be there. Now I needed to figure out my costume.

As an American at a Halloween party hosted by the U.S. Marines, I knew I had to really dress up. Luckily for me, one evening a few days before the party, I was out with Natalie and Sarah after work, and we decided as a group to dress up together. Our theme was "Hip-Hop."

Two days before the party, the three of us met in the old city in an area of the covered souq that's completely dedicated to textiles and clothes, with small shops spilling their material into the laneways. The laneways had been covered at some point with a metal roof to try keeping out the heat of the sun. You might think an old market would be selling only traditional Arab garb, but in reality, they sold everything.

In the small laneways of the old city, in the back alleys of the clothing souq, we found three matching velour tracksuits. It might sound like a strange find, but women in the Middle East love these velour tracksuits. They wear them around the house or sometimes even on the street.

The shop owner understood why Sarah and Natalie needed the tracksuits to walk around their house in style, but the shop owner was quite confused when I tried one on, especially when the back of the jacket said, in big and bold words, "Sexy Beautiful."

I told the shop owner I was trying it on for my sister—adding, "She was about my size," which made his eyes widen. At that point, the shop owner started laughing as I strutted around his small shop in a purple velour tracksuit. He sold us the tracksuits, and the three of us were now a trio of very good-looking hip-hop stars.

As Halloween approached, I had a costume, Amal was

coming to the party, and protesters were still protesting. The opposition labeled October 28 the "Friday of No-Fly Zone."

The opposition wanted the U.S. and others to enter into the Syrian conflict with more than just words—they wanted a "no-fly zone" like in Libya. It was reported by the opposition that thirty-six protestors were killed on that Friday, over one hundred wounded, and hundreds more arrested by the regime. It was also reported that seventeen regime soldiers were killed by the FSA.

The deaths and protests were now becoming commonplace to me. Reporting daily on violence had started to numb me. I no longer felt sick to my stomach when seeing pictures or videos of death. I was no longer shocked by what people could do to other people, and this concerned me. I guess being numb allowed me not to go crazy. It also maybe allowed me to justify to myself that it was okay for me to go to a Halloween party.

When the night of the party finally came. I started the night with my two other hip-hop stars at my apartment on the balcony, drinking and smoking cigarettes. Vuk, the Serbian diplomat, joined us. The four of us sat on the balcony having drinks and laughing about how ridiculous we looked in our sexy beautiful tracksuits.

While enjoying the cool night air, pregaming before the party, Amal messaged me and said she was getting ready. I asked what she was wearing, and she responded by saying I would have to wait and see. She added a smiley face at the end of the message, and my heart skipped a beat. I could not wait to see her, but at the same time, I was nervous. Since meeting her the first time, I had built her up in my head. Would we connect as we did the first time?

Just after nightfall, the four of us left my apartment and headed to the Marine house. The taxi driver who drove us to the party gave us a once-over, shaking his head in confusion as he drove us the short distance to the Embassy. I am sure he didn't know what to make of us.

As we spilled out of the taxi next to the U.S. Embassy, the Syrian security force members holding their AK-47s looked at us oddly too. Other guests were now arriving at the back door of the Embassy and entering the Marines' house. People were dressed as Vikings and kings, some people were in drag, others were vampires, and then there was Amal.

When I saw her, I stared. She looked wonderful. Amal could have stepped right out of a British pop culture photo spread with her outfit. She had fake tattoos, long extended eyelashes, and red lipstick. She was Amy Winehouse. I kind of felt my hip-hop costume was rather lame when compared to her.

As she walked up to us, our eyes met, but we both quickly looked away sheepishly. She then looked back at me and smiled, which lit up my world. For a second, I felt like it was just her and me standing there. But I snapped back into reality and introduced her to the others. Then we all stood in line and waited for the Marines to check IDs against the guest list.

Right after we entered the party, the Marine bar quickly filled up. It was a hell of a time, and all of the younger diplomats and most of the older ones still in Damascus all showed up. Additionally, foreign contacts and Syrian friends came.

This was not a formal diplomatic affair where people watched what they said or how much they drank. Shots were poured, and beers were pounded. Halloween parties always seem to make people a little crazier because they're in costume.

In the beginning, I tried to stay around Amal and spend time with her, but I was not good at standing still. The party was loud, and it was hard to talk. She also ran into people from the Western Embassy she worked at. Things for me were not going as planned. I wanted to talk to her. I regretted not asking her out on a proper date. A big party was not the place to get to know someone.

At some point, I left her with a drink and started to wander around the party, saying hello to people I knew and introducing myself to others. Eventually, I found myself sitting out back of the Marine house smoking cigarettes and laughing with a few other people in a small courtyard.

I had, it seemed, messed up because I was not spending any quality time with Amal. Past girlfriends described me as a social butterfly at parties. I would float around talking to everyone and ignoring them. That evening, I was no different.

I don't think Amal had a lousy time at the party as she always had a drink in her hand and spent most of the night talking and laughing with Lars, the most well-dressed diplomat from the Swedish Embassy. At some point later in the evening, as I was holding a drunken court on the back patio, Amal found me and said a quick goodbye.

When she said goodbye, she smiled at me, but it was not the same smile as the beginning of the night. She did not turn to look at me one more time like she did at 808. "Oh no," I thought to myself, "first I gave her my card instead of just asking for her number. Now I finally get to see her again, and I blow it."

Additionally, I felt a little jealous because she spent all night talking to Lars instead of me. It wasn't her fault; I was the social butterfly who didn't concentrate on her. By not doing so, did I give her the wrong vibe? Did she think I wasn't into her?

As she walked away, my gut flip-flopped in disgust at my inaction. Maybe I should have walked her out and made sure she got a taxi, but I didn't do that either. Instead, I waved goodbye from the patio.

After she left, I decided not to stress right then. If I blew it, I blew it. I was at a party, and I should enjoy it. Soon I found myself making air guitar moves on my back across the dance floor, and I realized I had smoked way too many cigarettes as my throat started to hurt. Eventually, I found myself outside of the Embassy inebriated and ready to go home.

I was ready to go home but had to stand there on the side of the street in my sexy tracksuit, waiting for a cab to pass by. The area around the Embassy was not full of bars or restaurants, so it seemed like I might have to stand there for some time. I contemplated walking home but decided against it.

Instead, I walked up to one of the Syrian security force regime guys with his AK-47 and asked him if I could have a cigarette. He gave me an odd look when I asked, but he then pulled out a pack of locally made, cheap, rough-tasting cigarettes, handed me one, and took one out for himself.

He lit the cigarette for me as I held it in my lips, and then he lit his own. We did not say anything to one another but stood there smoking, watching cars drive by. I am sure drivers were confused as they passed us. It cannot be every night that someone sees an armed Syrian Regime gunman standing next to a drunk Western man in a purple velour tracksuit.

There we were, two people on opposite sides of a revolution. Just two people enjoying cigarettes. One with a gun and the other with a soon-to-be hangover getting along on a Damascus street. I remember thinking, "If we can stand here in peace, breathing in the night air together, why can't the world get along? Why can't we all just chill out for a minute?"

As the cigarette burned down to the butt, I looked the Syrian Security member in the eyes and nodded to him a "thanks for the cig" gesture, to which he nodded back a "no problem." I dropped the cigarette butt to the ground and stepped on it before flagging down a taxi.

On my way home in the backseat of a taxi, I was a little confused by how the night had gone. I played back the night's jokes, conversations, and stories. But by the time I arrived home and crawled into bed, still with my tracksuit on, I was only wondering if I had blown it with Amal.

CHAPTER 20

Friday Drives

I WOKE UP THE DAY AFTER HALLOWEEN thinking about the night before and battling a headache. I'd had a great time at the party, but a horrible "date" with Amal. Lying in bed that morning, I made up my mind: I needed to ask her out on a real date.

Yet, in my next message to her, I didn't ask her out. No, instead I said that I loved her costume of Amy Winehouse. I knew I wanted to ask her out, but I was afraid I would be rejected after such a poor showing at the party.

Even so, thinking of her made me smile as the sunlight filled my room. A phone call interrupted my daydream of a first date with her. It was time to get back to work.

I was not sure of my work schedule over the next few weeks. Without Ambassador Ford around, I wondered if daily work would change. The person now leading the Embassy was the Deputy Chief of Mission (DCM), Patrick Moran, who had taken over the leadership role of the Embassy.

Moran was an old-school diplomat and had arrived in Damascus just a week or two after I arrived in August. However, he had served at Embassy Damascus before, thirty-plus years ago, and even married a Syrian lady during his first tour there. The big difference between Moran and Ford was that Moran never seemed in a rush and was not going to rock the boat.

Even if Moran was not going to stir the pot like Ford, the revolution was going to continue, and we were going to have to keep on reporting. One way we got information for the sitrep was the Friday drive around. It might sound like a nice Sunday drive, but, in reality, those drives were trying.

Friday drives entailed me and a few other people getting an Embassy car and driving around for a few hours to try and witness the protests. We wanted to understand the scope and size of the opposition. People said protests were happening, and I would watch videos of them, but we needed to confirm it with our own eyes.

At the beginning of the uprising, there were large protests in Damascus, but now those huge events had stopped. As we drove around, I could see why. We observed swarms of riot police all suited up, ready to respond to protestors. They would be sitting under the overpasses, avoiding the Arab sun while being close to buses that were ready and waiting to drive them out and crush a protest.

Another reason large protests no longer occurred was that the regime had done an excellent job at rounding up opposition members. Many Syrians who were opposed to the regime were vanishing into the Syrian prison system. Sometimes they would pop back up alive, and other times bodies would show up in the morgues for their families to claim. Other times, they just vanished. This meant many of the local organizers of the first protests were either hiding, in jail, or dead, or they had fled the country.

On November 4, the "Friday of God is Greatest" protests, I did not see any protests in downtown Damascus. I did not physically see the twenty-plus protesters reported killed by the regime. I did not personally see the hundreds of bodies brought into hospitals during the first week of November. Instead, I watched videos and saw pictures while staring at my computer screen.

Not all of our Friday drives went smoothly. Once, after looking at Syrian security forces under an overpass, our car was chased down by two cops on motorbikes. We were pulled over, and all of us sat there wondering what was going to happen. The cop nervously talked to us through our closed window, and I had images of being dragged out of the car and searched. Luckily, once the cop found out we were diplomats, he let us go.

Another time, our car got stopped at a checkpoint by two members of the security service. They thought we had come from one of the outlying Damascus suburbs, which were becoming opposition strongholds, so they would not let our car leave the checkpoint. Even after they took our diplomatic IDs, they would not let us depart. A few guys continually walked around our car with AK-47s at the ready.

Another security member noisily talked to his boss on the phone, asking what he should do with us. At some point, one of the other people in the car with me said, "Get ready to be arrested."

I had never been arrested in my life. I have never been

handcuffed. That Friday, sitting at the checkpoint, I thought it would happen. The faces of the Syrian security guys who stopped us were not smiling. I didn't think those guys would let me bum a cigarette.

I started thinking about all the stories I'd heard of Syrians getting stopped by the regime at checkpoints. They would be taken from their cars and disappear. They would be vanished into small, cramped cells only to be brought out for torture sessions to extract information and guilty pleas. Their innocence did not matter. Their fate was sealed with a bullet or a noose. Eventually, they would be buried in mass graves or cremated in government furnaces. Many families would never know what happened.

Let me say, "I am fortunate." About thirty minutes after we were stopped, one of the Syrian security guys at the checkpoint walked over to the car and handed our papers back. We all looked at one another and smiled. Maybe getting our papers back was a good sign.

A little later, the guy that had been on the phone walked over and just said, "Yallah" or "let's go" in Arabic slang. With a wave of his hand, we left the checkpoint. As we drove away, there was a collective sigh from everyone in the car.

I think we all knew we were lucky. The regime could have killed us—dumped our bodies somewhere and blamed some terrorists for our disappearance. We could have gone missing in the secret Syrian prisons, never to be seen or heard of again like so many others.

CHAPTER 21

Date Night

AFTER STRESSFUL MOMENTS LIKE THE FRIDAY DRIVES, why did I find it so difficult to ask Amal on a date? I was happy to put my body in harm's way but not my feelings. However, after a few bad days at work, I decided that I had nothing to lose. I should just ask her out. I found the courage and sent Amal the message asking her to go to dinner with me. It felt like I was in high school again, messaging a girl and waiting for her response. Every time my phone made a noise, I held my breath, wondering if she had responded with a yes.

Eventually, the message popped up on my phone. It was from Amal, and she said dinner would be great. I sat there smiling at my phone. Now I just needed to figure out where we would get dinner.

As we both waited for Thursday to arrive, we continued to message each other. I said she looked cute in her new Facebook profile picture dressed up as Amy Winehouse. She responded by saying that my profile picture also looked cute. As Thursday got closer, I started to think, "Hmm, maybe this girl does like me."

Work that week included more tragedy in the daily sitreps. More reports of arrests, shootings, torture. Areas around Homs were continuing to heat up with daily reports of clashes and deaths. Opposition activities and leaders started to call the world's attention to the city as it slowly turned into a war zone. The hope I had for meaningful peace and reforms seemed to be vanishing.

Friday, November 11, was deemed the "Friday of Freezing Syria's Arab League Membership." Outside of Syria, it seemed the SNC and others were trying to isolate the regime on the world's stage. The opposition wanted to replace the regime at those international organizations and hoped they could somehow become the official government of Syria by doing so.

As moves were made on the international scene, I was no longer looking forward to going to the office and doing sitreps, even if they were important. There was little to nothing I could look forward to—just more deaths, arrests, violence, and sadness. Amal's responses to my messages and the prospect of a date with her became the only positive thing in my days.

We decided to meet on a Thursday night at Bab Sharqi, the old city's eastern gate. The plan was to meet at the gate and wander through the ancient city together. I told her we would find a restaurant or bar to stop in and enjoy dinner and drinks.

I was hoping Amal already had a place in mind. I wanted to see which place she chose so I could somehow understand more of who she was. Would she go fancy or basic, pricey or cheap, Western or Syrian food?

We were meeting on a Thursday because it was the start of

the weekend. I had to work on Friday, but at least Amal did not. I had promised myself before heading out that I was not going to worry about work. I was taking a mental vacation. I was going on a date with a lovely and beautiful woman.

Walking through a Roman arched gate into an ancient city to meet a beautiful woman at dusk was magical. As I entered, I saw her standing there. She looked stunning in the light of the setting sun. She did not dress to impress like some women in the Middle East or New York City. No low-cut cleavage line or a miniskirt. She wore long pants and a long-sleeve shirt. She was not glammed-up with layers of makeup, so her natural beauty radiated out when she smiled.

As I approached her, I could not help but smile. I greeted her with a "hello, you look wonderful." To which she responded with a smile and a blush.

With that, we turned together and started walking. We did not walk hand in hand or arm in arm as we set off. We walked side by side while we wandered through the small laneways and alleys, sometimes walking one behind the other when someone was coming the other way.

As we explored the old city, we also explored each other through conversation. Just like on our first encounter, it was effortless and fun. Amal pointed things out in the old city streets. Little cafes, small bars, and old shops. She shared memories of times past spent in this area of town with her friends. Back when she said things were normal. However, we did not stray away from a light conversation, full of laughter. For both of us, the evening was an escape into the ancient city.

Eventually, we both grew hungry, and we decided to enter a nice Syrian restaurant. I had thought restaurants would be crowded on a Thursday night, but due to the faltering Syrian economy, the place we stopped at was almost empty. Only a few diners were sitting around candle-lit tables on the dark rooftop of the old Damascus riad.

Sitting with Amal in the evening air, we looked at one another across the table. She looked even more gorgeous now than when we met early in the night. The walk had taken some of the nervousness away from both of us.

That evening we talked about where we were both from — she from Damascus and me from Ohio. We talked about our families. She had one older sister, while I was the middle child with two brothers. We talked about what we each studied — Amal literature and me history.

We touched on so many subjects that first evening, but we did not delve deeply into them. Maybe we were trying to figure out how two people from very different backgrounds could feel connected. Perhaps we were just going through the motions of a first date and checking the boxes of questions to figure out how the other one came to be.

I found out she had been to the U.S. once before to visit her cousins, but overall she had not traveled much. I found out she had a deep love for music and books. I was shocked that she had such a deep knowledge of English/American music. She loved English-speaking bands and English novels.

By the end of the evening, though, it was clear to me that Amal was a bright, cute, and strong Syrian woman. More importantly, I started to fall in love with her laughter. In a time of sadness, I found her true-hearted laugh such an intoxicating sound. I was overwhelmed by the way she turned her head when trying to control her laugh and smile.

I don't remember how the food was or what we had to drink. I don't remember paying the bill or even talking to the waiter that evening. My eyes, ears, and thoughts were all concentrated on Amal. To put it simply, I was smitten.

I am not sure what time it was when it was time to leave. I am sure we sat there long after we finished our meals and drinks. Eventually, it was time to go.

I paid, and we strolled back to Bab Sharqi. The streets were darker now and lit by street lamps. We still walked side by side, and I thought about trying to hold her hand but sheepishly did not.

Once we exited the ancient city gate, we paused and looked at each other. We smiled and neither of us wanted the night to end, but this night would not go further. Instead, I told her I had a wonderful time, and she nodded in agreement. I told her we should do it again soon, and she said a definitive "yes!"

She then walked over and hugged me goodbye. It was a quick hug that I wished would have been a long embrace. I wanted to pull her close and kiss her that evening. I wanted to be close to her. I wanted to feel her breath. However, standing on a Damascus street was not the place for any of that.

The hug ended quickly, and we stood across from one another, smiling and blushing. I think we both knew we wanted more, but that wasn't going to happen. Instead, we both headed off to our separate cars and our separate homes. She went to her parent's apartment, and I went to my large, lonely apartment.

The following day, I got up early and headed to the Embassy. I wrote up the daily sitrep. Protests and clashes continued in many different areas of Syria. Syrian activists estimate that this Friday, thirty civilians were killed by regime forces.

The opposition's theme about Syria leaving the Arab League came true on November 12 because the Arab League announced that Syria was suspended. The Arab countries and the West now seemed aligned against the regime, at least diplomatically. However, even if they all now condemned the violent actions of the Assad Regime, no one knew how, or at least no one agreed on how to push the Assad Regime out of Syria.

But the Assad Regime did know how to react to the Arab League and sent its mob of thugs in government buses to attack embassies in Damascus and consulates in other Syrian cities. This included the Qatari, Saudi, and Turkish Embassies.

On that day I watched from the U.S. Embassy as a pro-regime mob rushed the Turkish Embassy located only a few hundred yards away from us. The regime sent in a fire truck to spray water at the protesters, but the fire truck quickly ran out of water and left. Just like a mob had done to the U.S. Embassy a few months before, the Turkish Embassy and the other embassies and consulates had some shattered windows and some damage, but they were still left standing.

I was shocked the mob did not continue up the street to attack us again because it would have been easy to do. All of the U.S. Embassy's security team was ready to go, but, again, there is little an embassy can do against hundreds or thousands of people if they decide to attack. I guess the mob of government thugs and supporters did not have those orders that day.

A statement from the Turkish Foreign Ministry about the attacks stated, "It is surely meaningful that these attacks happened after an Arab League decision on Syria and were the strongest and most frequent on the Turkish missions." The statement added, "Turkey is not even a member of the Arab League."

Even if Turkey was not a member of the Arab League, it was the home base for the SNC and thus a target for the Syrians. If the Syrian opposition was going to be based in Turkey, then the regime would not be friendly with them.

The diplomatic world was getting smaller and smaller. The regime made the diplomatic world know it could reach out and touch you. Even if the Assad Regime held back against diplomats, it was not holding back its forces from attacking Syrians. By this time in November, the UN estimated 3,500 people had been killed since the start of the revolution.

CHAPTER 22

Getting to Know

THAT FIRST DATE WITH AMAL ALLOWED ME TO FEEL NORMAL. Over those first few months, I had felt many emotions as I watched Syria tear itself apart, but the one feeling that I missed the most was feeling normal.

I think it is hard to describe feeling normal. I guess it's the feeling of being comfortable in your own skin. The feeling you get when you wake up at your parents' house in your childhood bed and know your mom is making breakfast. The way you know your way around your hometown without looking at a map. It's the feeling of being so familiar with something that you know it without thinking about it.

Amal became a drug or an elixir that calmed me and took me to an ordinary place. Even if we did not see each other every day, I could get sips of her throughout the day via her messages. Amal's messages to me represented something normal in my twilight zone. Her messages were not about revolution but about a song or a book she had read.

Looking back at the early messages between us, I pushed the

communication. I would ask her to send me a song each day.

She was so into music that I figured it was a good idea, even though I am not a music aficionado. I like classic rock songs and tend to play them over and over again. Sad, I know. But I started listening to new music for her and figuring out who she was through the daily songs she sent me.

Unlike me, Amal was particular about her songs. She wanted to have them tell a story and be listened to at the right time and in the proper order. I found her passion for music charming, and I saw she used music to project her inner feelings.

At first, she tended to share sad songs from bands like Radiohead. I would respond by sharing happy songs by classic rock bands. Those first weeks together, we shared song after song and somehow got closer via other people's words. It was kind of like in the 90s or 2000s when people gave their significant other a mixed tape or a mixed CD.

In those weeks after our first date, we bonded through messages and songs. We only spoke a few times over the phone in early November, and they were not long and meaningful conversations. Instead, I just waited for little messages of joy from her.

Our dating started in these messages. Even though we were in the same city, we both found it hard to see one another. Work was too busy for me. I was busy trying to figure out what the hell was happening in this revolution, which was making its way into a civil war supported by opposition figures and proxies abroad.

By mid-November, things were not looking on the up and up on the diplomatic front of ending this revolution peacefully or diplomatically. We and others were implementing more sanctions, and Syria was suffering economically, but the regime was still there and in power.

Regional leaders were trying to urge Assad to leave, but the regime responded through violence—the only way they knew. Jordan's King Abdullah criticized the Assad Regime on TV and said Assad should step down. The result of the king's words was a November 15 attack on the Jordanian Embassy by a mob of Assad thugs.

On November 16, the French Ambassador, Eric Chevalier, also left Syria as Ford had done. Ford and his French buddy, who had pushed for diplomatic solutions to the problems in Syria, were both now gone. The revolution was now spinning toward the abyss, and the opposition and the regime started to build allies for a bloody civil war.

The Gulf countries, European countries, Turkey, and the U.S. moved to line up behind the opposition on the world stage. The Assad Regime was looking to its few partners in crime for help, including Russia and Iran. It might seem like a lopsided list of allies, but allies are only as good as how much they support you and what domestic political risks they are willing to take to be on your side.

I, on the other hand, was not in the lofty world of international diplomacy. I was not in Paris having meetings or at the UN in New York pushing some resolution. I was on the ground talking to real people. I was living the revolution.

My meetings in Damascus were a little different, and they were getting harder and harder to arrange because Syrians were becoming more nervous. Many Syrians were fleeing the country out of fear of arrest and death. Not just opposition members were leaving; Damascus was also emptying of young Syrians with connections abroad.

It seemed every young Syrian was looking for work anywhere other than in Syria. There were questions about U.S. visas daily. The brain drain of conflict nations was happening en masse in Syria by November 2011. The young, the educated, the multinationals, the connected people, the super-rich—they were all leaving. From my apartment, I saw fewer lights in apartments around me as more and more people left.

The Syrians leaving at this time were not the people who later became refugees in the UN camps. These were the educated elite who were leaving to pursue jobs in major companies. They could get a work visa. They had the money for a plane ticket. These were the people who had been driving an economically stable Syria before the uprising. They were people like Amal and her friends.

As the rich and connected left Syria, the international community repeatedly failed in its attempts to avoid civil war. The people that remained in Syria would be the ones that would face the coming storm. All I kept on thinking was that one of those people was Amal.

CHAPTER 23

Street Corners

IT WAS SAD TO SEE AND HEAR ABOUT PEOPLE LEAVING because they saw no future in Syria, but it was more heartbreaking to see people flee in fear of the regime. Those people wanted to stay in Syria but, rightfully so, feared death at the hands of the regime. I believe that if Syrians were meeting with me during this time, they were the bravest of the brave, as I am sure meeting with an American diplomat did not bring you into the good graces of the Assad Regime.

Even if it was getting harder, I was still going to meetings. They were just becoming a little more tainted with "stranger danger." One time, I got an email asking to meet with a person, but I was not given an address or a phone number for the meeting. I was told to meet on a street corner in central Damascus.

It is not customary in diplomacy to agree to attend a meeting on a street corner with someone you do not know. I told myself, well, this is not a regular time for anyone at the Embassy, so maybe this is what I should do. Additionally, I was told to meet people by Ambassador Ford. People were becoming so nervous about meeting with the "Americans" that they would not openly invite me into their home or book a table at a public restaurant.

Diplomats are not trained on street corner meetings, but I figured if someone wanted to meet on a street corner, I shouldn't show up there in a suit and tie in my diplomatically plated car. For this reason, I left work way ahead of the agreed meeting time. I went home and changed out of my fancy clothes into street clothes that any average Syrian could have. I left my car at my apartment, took a taxi to another area of town, walked around, and had a coffee. Then I took another random taxi to the corner.

I had no idea if this would effectively prevent someone from tailing me to this meeting. I still have no idea if I should have done it this way. I just knew that the people I'd met with before were suddenly gone after I saw them. Maybe they were arrested, perhaps they fled, or maybe they were warned not to meet with me again.

Now, concerning the street corner people, they had reached out and were willing to meet with a U.S. diplomat, but by just giving me a street corner, they were also making it clear they were trying to mitigate their risk.

If they were willing to risk meeting with me, I felt like I should also take the risk and meet with them. I asked my bosses, and they did not object. So, I set off on my roundabout way to the street corner for a meeting.

There I was, standing on a street corner smoking a cigarette, waiting for someone to stop and talk to me. The meeting time came and went, and I decided to spend a few more minutes on the corner before walking away. A few people passed me as I stood there, but none of them made eye contact with me, and none approached. Just before I was about to give up and head home, a woman in her twenties strolled past me and said quietly, "Come with me."

We walked away from the street corner and down the block a little way. I thought we would go to a cafe, or maybe an apartment or a house. Instead, the young lady stopped next to a car and jumped into the front seat. There was a man in the driver's seat not much older than her. As she got into the car, she motioned for me to get in the back seat.

Looking back, getting into the back of that car was kind of crazy. Maybe I shouldn't have done it, but my risk tolerance was high at the time, and I thought, "Well, perhaps we will just have the meeting in the car. That would be safe."

So, I got into the back seat of a random car. Right after I got into the car, the driver started the engine, and we pulled out into traffic on the street. "Crap," I thought to myself. "This is how people get kidnapped and killed. This is how I get my head cut off by some jihadi group of terrorists."

As we moved through the Damascus streets, a lump formed in my throat as I wondered where the heck we were going. The only odd comfort I had was that I didn't have a black bag over my head.

After driving for a few minutes in silence, the driver and the lady in the front seat started to laugh. It was one of those nervous laughs which relieves stress. It did not sound like an evil laugh which would have caused me to worry. Instead, it made the lump in my throat go away.

The woman then turned around in the front seat and smiled back at me. She then said in English, "Sorry I was late to get you. We were both looking at you and trying to figure out if you were an American Diplomat or Shabiha."

Shabiha is Arabic for "ghost," the nickname for the regime's thugs—a regime mafia-type since the 1980s. Before the uprising, these guys ran smuggling rings in and out of Syria. This mafia was started by members of the Assad family who recruited the Shabiha members from the Alawite religious minority that the Assad family comes from.

When the revolution started, the Shabiha began transitioning into militias to help crush the uprising. Around Damascus, I could recognize them because these guys drove around in nice cars with whited-out car plates. Their plates let everyone know, even the cops, don't mess with me.

The Shabiha also liked looking the part of a mafioso. Some wore leather jackets and dark shades. They usually had a cigarette hanging from their mouths. They had short hair, long beards, and looked like they liked hitting the gym.

When the lady joked that they thought I might have been a Shabiha, it made perfect sense. I had on a leather jacket. I was smoking a cigarette. I had short hair, a beard, and was slightly muscular. I guess I did look like a light-skinned Alawite mafia regime-loving thug.

When she told me this in the car, it brought a smile to my face. Inside I was laughing hysterically, but outside I only let out a small chuckle and smiled. The whole car seemed a bit more relaxed. After that, they both introduced themselves and explained where we were going. I was pretty sure these were good people, and I was not going to lose my head on video. It was an immense feeling of relief.

We drove quickly through the Damascus streets. The driver seemed to drive aimlessly through the city's streets, and he looked around constantly to see if we were being followed. Maybe we were, perhaps we were not. I don't know.

Eventually, he must have been satisfied that no one was following us because we pulled up to an old apartment building, and they told me our meeting would take place there. I had already gone on a car ride with them and was alive, so I might as well go into the apartment.

We parked the car and walked quickly into the apartment building. We were in an area of the city I did not know well, but judging by the building we had entered, it was a typical middle-class area of town. After going up a few flights of stairs, we entered an apartment.

Once inside, I was introduced to a few more people, and we started the actual meeting. Like all meetings in Damascus, there was a lot of coffee, cigarettes, and talk. After some time, our discussions came to an end, and I got up to leave.

I did not get a ride back with the people who had picked me up. I decided during the meeting that it might be better if I left by myself and walked for a while before getting a taxi back to the Embassy. It seemed like everyone had an idea of how not to raise the attention of the Syrian security services. I would not argue about how we should or should not avoid being arrested or killed, so I said okay and got up to leave.

I shook hands and said goodbye to everyone in the apartment when one guy showed me a stack of papers and instructed me to take them to the Embassy. I said okay, and he gave them to me.

In an ordinary world, I would have just walked out with papers in hand. However, I was not in an ordinary world. If someone was watching the apartment, I didn't think leaving with papers would look good for anyone. So, after he handed me the papers, I stuffed them down my pants. The guy that gave me the papers saw what I had done and gave me a thumbs up. As I left, I smiled at him with a fake smile which I hope translated to, "Thanks, and these papers better be important."

As I walked down the random Damascus street, I tried not to walk like I had paper stuffed into my underwear. It was not a comfortable, joyful walk, but after a few miles and two different taxis, my paper-stuffed underwear ass made it back to the Embassy.

I am happy to say this was the only meeting I had while in Damascus when I had to stuff paper down my pants. However, meetings with most Syrians during the revolution were stressful because they were risking so much by talking to me. They were risking their well-being, their freedom, and their lives. Me stuffing papers down my pants or getting into random cars seemed like the least I could do to decrease the risk.

My life in Syria had become all about risk. My life was about managing risk, but that was difficult to do because it seemed that the risks and challenges of work were becoming more significant day by day.

I could risk very little if I just stayed in the Embassy all the time and wrote cables based on internet searches and Facebook posts. I risked more by going out to get information, but I knew it was needed.

I also knew I need to risk more in my personal life, I also needed to risk my emotions with Amal. I guess when you risk your health and safety in a revolution, you are also willing to risk heartbreak.

CHAPTER 24

Listening

DIPLOMATS IN SYRIA WERE ALL WONDERING how long this revolution would last. Was it over? Was it a civil war? Had peaceful approaches failed? Was diplomacy dead for now, and would it only start again as peace negotiations at the end of a civil war?

These were some of the questions I would hear diplomats debate while sitting around having drinks at 808 or on someone's veranda. Everyone knew things were getting worse, but Western diplomats tended to maintain hope. In contrast, others were already confident that a civil war was the only stage to debate Syria's future.

While diplomats sat around Damascus pondering the future, the Syrian opposition called their November 18 day of protests the "Friday of the Expulsion of the Ambassadors." They wanted countries to expel the Syrian Ambassadors, which would show which countries stood with or against the Assad Regime. However, if a country did kick out the Syrian Ambassador, it would lead to the Assad Regime expelling that country's ambassador in Damascus.

It seemed that if everyone started expelling ambassadors and diplomats, we would all have decided war was the answer. The regime had already committed to the route of violence as their solution to stopping the revolution—and if sanctions and resolutions were not effective at reforming or toppling the regime, the opposition was saying it would also pick up arms to bring about change. On that Friday, the opposition said that regime forces killed at least twenty people.

When sitting with diplomats, we did not always discuss Syria. Sitting with Vuk over a drink or two, we would talk about our lives. It seemed I was not the only person that was attempting to date someone during a revolution.

For Vuk and Natalie, their dating life was a little easier because neither of them are Syrian. That is not to say the UK and Serbia are the same, but at least neither of them were from a country that was currently crumbling. Nevertheless, they shared the same issue of not knowing the future. Their lives were unstable. They could, like me, be told to leave Syria at a moment's notice. However, Vuk always noted that he was not going anywhere, even if there was fighting in downtown Damascus, because living in Belgrade had given him a very high risk tolerance.

I was more stressed than Vuk because, up until Syria, my life was relatively stable. I had never lived in a country that was falling apart. I had the American can-do attitude. If there was a problem, I could fix it.

However, Vuk helped me realize that sometimes you cannot fix everything. Some things are just bigger than you, and you are just along for the ride. Vuk made this point time and again over drinks when he would say, "What can you do?"

When he said those words, they really were not a question. They were a statement that caused us both to shrug our shoulders and take a drink of our Black Label.

He had a valid point. What could I do to change things? I could send cable after cable, sitrep after sitrep, but were those going to change the trajectory of Syria? I should not fool myself into thinking that I had that kind of power. Instead, I started thinking, "What should I do?" I should just live my life. If diplomacy was failing, I was winning on the dating front.

Now more than ever, I was finding my messages with Amal the only pleasure in my day, and we finally decided to see each other again. This time we did not go out. This time we decided to meet at my apartment.

Because most single people in Syria still live with their parents, having my own apartment where we could spend time together was a luxury for two single people in Damascus. Usually, unmarried Syrian couples have to spend their entire dating life at cafes, on park benches, or in their cars. We were lucky because we could have our date in private. Well, kind of in private.

Amal came over after work sometime between five and six. When I opened the door to my apartment, she flashed me such a huge smile that my heart skipped as she walked through my front door.

As she came in, she took one look around and started to laugh. She then turned to me and asked, "Do you really live here by yourself?"

It was a valid question because my apartment was meant to

house a huge extended family, and instead of six to eight people in the apartment, it was just me. To her, it seemed like a waste of space.

"It's just me," I responded. We walked from empty room to empty room. Each time we entered a new room, she would laugh and shake her head again.

After the tour, I grabbed a bottle of rosé and some food from the kitchen, and we headed to the front balcony.

The conversation again flowed easily between us as we sat there sipping our wine. I was again taken with the feeling of normal. The stresses around us seemed to fall off the balcony as we sat there watching the sun slip below the city's skyline.

Once the sun descended and darkness crept in, Amal and I went inside. I figured she would be going home soon, but she suggested listening to some music. We found ourselves lying on the apartment floor listening to music selected by Amal.

Before she played each song, she would tell me about the artist and what she wanted me to listen for. After each song ended, she wanted to hear from me about what I thought about it. She would ask, "How did that make you feel?" "Did you like it? "What do you think they meant by that lyric?"

I would answer as best I could, but to be honest, I was not paying attention to the music. I was lost in Amal's excitement for the music. I was lost in her smile and eyes as she looked at me. My feelings for her that night were more substantial than my responses to her questions, so eventually, I just fell silent, lying on the floor with her. We made a little bubble of normal that was fragile because I knew we were not alone.

When I had moved into the apartment in Al Malky, I had requested internet at my new apartment, and one of the local Syrian IT guys at the Embassy told me he would help.

However, weeks passed, and my home internet was not working. I thought, "Well, maybe this takes time in Syria." I also thought that perhaps the locally employed IT staffer was busy, so it might take time to get it running. Eventually, I went to talk to him and ask about my internet status.

When I entered his office, he looked at me and smiled like there was no issue in the world. I sat down and asked him about the internet, and he said clearly that day, "I would be happy to help, but I don't want to put the internet in your specific apartment."

I found this slightly disturbing, so I asked him, "What's wrong with my apartment?" I knew every other U.S. diplomat had the internet in their place. What was wrong with my place? Why would the Embassy put me into an apartment which could not get the internet?

His response to my question was that my apartment was near some of the security offices of the Syrian security agencies, and it made him uncomfortable. That made sense to me, but at the same time, the other people at the Embassy all had internet at their apartments, and many also lived near me, so I thought having Syrian security agencies nearby should not be an issue.

I looked at him and pleaded with him to go to my apartment and just see if he could get the internet turned on. I told him that if at any point he felt uncomfortable once he was there, he could leave.

I wanted to talk to my parents and friends in the U.S. from my apartment. I did not want to do this at cafes anymore. I wanted to write emails from home. I wanted the freedom the internet offers.

After my pleading, he agreed to help and said he would try to turn on the internet at my apartment. I thanked him and left his office to finish the sitrep.

When I got home from work that same day, to my surprise, the internet was working. The IT guy had come to my apartment, and the internet was working! It had been months since I had the internet at home, and I did a small dance in my apartment to celebrate. When I got to work the next day, I went directly to the IT guy's office to thank him.

I walked into his office, offered him my thanks, and told him I was grateful for the help. After I thanked him, he leaned over to my ear and whispered, "You already had three live internet connections in your house. I was not afraid to turn yours on but to accidentally turn off one of the others."

After he leaned back away from my ear, his words struck home. My apartment was not private when I closed and locked the door. Syrian security services were there every day with me. I always assumed the regime could listen and was listening to my calls and following me when I was out and about, and I figured my apartment was not a place for work conversations.

After that conversation with the IT guy, though, I knew for sure the Assad Regime was in my apartment with me.

So as I laid there on the floor with Amal in my apartment listening to music, some Syrian security guy or guys were sitting in a small office somewhere down the street listening too. We had a third wheel with us that night in the apartment.

I did not particularly care if the Regime was listening as long as we stayed away from certain topics. I would not want to talk to Amal about my work, the revolution, the regime, or anything else that could endanger her. I believed that as long as we stayed on topics like music, nothing bad could come from it. I just hoped the regime security guy liked Amal's choices in music as much as I did.

It got later and later as we lay on the floor listening to Amal's playlist. Amal then turned to me and said she was tired but did not want to go home yet. She asked me to wake her up in thirty minutes and curled up next to me. I told her I would wake her. With that, she closed her eyes and drifted off as music softly played.

With Amal curled up under my arm, I looked at the ceiling and smiled. I was not comfortable on the floor, but Amal was next to me. After a few minutes, I shut my eyes as well.

Before I knew it, Amal was shaking me and asked, "Why did you not wake me?"

Oh no, I thought to myself as I looked at my watch. More than thirty minutes had passed, and it was now well after midnight. All I could do was look at her and say, "I'm sorry."

She responded by giving me a look that said, "I forgive you… but next time, you have to wake me."

As we got up off the floor, she lamented that her mom would be distraught as it was not expected or condoned for a Syrian woman to spend the night away from home. Syrian parents expected their daughters, no matter their age, to come home at night.

I said I understood as I walked her to the front door and opened it for her. As she left, she turned and said, "See you soon," before rushing onto the elevator.

As she departed from my sight she entered my thoughts. I got into bed by myself. She had traveled from my eyes to my heart, which made going to bed alone that night a little more bearable.

CHAPTER 25

College Party

I WAS A LITTLE NERVOUS WHEN I WOKE UP the following day because I wondered what Amal told her mother and father. I hoped
her late-night arrival home had not caused her any significant
issues. At the same time, I was smiling when I got up because I
had gotten to sleep next to her. I hoped the Syrian security guy
or girl listening to us snoring enjoyed it.

Later in the day, I got a message from Amal to let me know
she told her parents she had fallen asleep at a girlfriend's house
during a movie, and they were none the wiser.

It would have been nice not to worry about parents since we
were both in our mid-twenties. It seemed strange to be sneaking
around at this stage in life, but I guess I had to adjust to the dating
culture of the Middle East. At the same time, I tried to bring some
U.S. culture to Syria.

Having Amal over was wonderful, but she was not the first
person I'd had over. Every once in a while, Sarah, Natalie, and
Vuk would come over for drinks on the balcony. During one of
those evenings, we got to talking about U.S. college parties. Their

big question was, "Are the big, epic college parties shown in U.S. movies real?" My simple answer was, "Yes."

Most of the world knows about U.S. college parties through movies and TV shows. Foreigners know about frat houses, *Animal House*, and drinking. There is a definite stereotype of universities in the United States, and I decided I would reinforce all of them.

Also, it kind of felt like it was my turn to play host in Damascus. Over previous weekends, I attended a few small parties at a few other diplomats' houses and UN workers' houses. None of them were crazy wild, but they were fun, and I thought I should repay them by hosting a party of my own.

In mid-November, I started spreading the word of a party at my place. The theme was "College Night." I told everyone I'd met about it and told them to invite others. "I have a big apartment," I thought; I could fit a few hundred people in there.

I wanted people to extend the invite because I had no idea how many people would show up. The worst thing in the world is hosting a party no one comes to. I did not want to invite Amal and her friends to a party that would be empty.

As the date got closer and closer, it seemed clear to me the word was spreading—more and more people seemed to have heard about it. People would text me and ask. "Do you mind if I also tell Fredick about the party?" I would respond to every message asking about adding people to the guest list with the same response, "Sure, everyone is welcome."

I was happy to invite the world, but as the date for the party got closer and closer, I had done little to nothing to prepare for the party other than telling people there would be one.

I was too busy with work and trying to figure how capitals were creating their Syrian policies as they just seemed to be created out of thin air. For example, toward the end of November, the French Foreign Minister Alain Juppé started talking about "humanitarian corridors." The term sounded nice, but what did it actually mean in Syria?

He had raised the humanitarian corridor idea after it became clear the opposition parts of Homs were now under siege, with no food, medicine, or water reaching the areas surrounded by the regime's forces.

After the diplomatic world and media got buzzing about the idea of "humanitarian corridors," I was told to go and talk to the other diplomats to see if they had a plan for this. So, I went over and spoke to a few diplomats. They all said, "Listen, we have no idea where this idea came from. There is no plan. The Foreign Minister just said it, and now we are trying to make a plan."

Ideas are constantly made up back in capitals. Talking points are created for good sound bites. Politicians talk, the media publishes headlines, and before you know it, there are a few words that sound good next to one another. Those few words convey some type of meaning for large populations to figure out.

The problem is that there is often no plan to take those few words and do things on the ground. I mean, did people really think that in the middle of a siege, when the regime was purposefully trying to starve and crush the spirits of opposition forces and civilians, they were going to let supplies through the lines? The answer was straightforward—no, the regime was not going to let that happen.

The regime knew it was in the fight for its life. Assad and the regime members had chosen to start a civil war instead of doing reforms. They were going to be brutal as the international community kept putting them in corners. They would do what it took to beat the opposition because Assad and others didn't want to end up like Gaddafi, killed on the side of some random road while hiding in a drainage pipe.

It was now clear that the regime had chosen civil war, and the opposition needed an army. Protestors labeled November 25 the "Friday of the Free Syrian Army is Protecting Me." On that day, the Free Syrian Army reported that it attacked a military base in Homs province and killed ten regime soldiers.

The Syrian civil war was becoming more real every day, but capitals still felt the war could be avoided. Somehow, they thought the regime would allow aid to the "rebels." That somehow the Regime would say, "You're right, those people are starving. Stop dropping bombs and bring in the food. Look at that nice humanitarian corridor."

As the world was trying to come up with creative new terms to solve the problems in Syria, I was going to have a party. It seemed appropriate that people on the front lines of diplomacy, who were working almost every day of the week, should get a chance to blow off some steam.

As the party approached, Amal and I continued to text every day. She was excited about the party, and I was looking forward to playing host to everyone. I thought having a huge party would impress her in some odd way, and I wanted to impress her. I wanted her to think I was cool. That I knew a lot of people. I guess

I wanted to show her that I was popular.

From the moment I met Amal, I was trying to impress her when she was not around. I felt like my messages needed to be crisper, texts with jokes funnier, and my song choices more thoughtful. However, when we were together, I did not feel the stress to impress. I didn't need to be funnier, smarter, or wiser than I really was, I could just be naturally normal Shawn.

However, leading up to the party, we were not together, so my stress to impress was real. I also committed myself to only being somewhat of a social butterfly once the party started. I did not want to make the same mistake I'd made a few weeks earlier at Halloween.

The day of the party finally arrived, and I started preparations. Before I went out to buy things I asked myself, "What does a college party need? The answer: lots of beer and games.

Beer and ice was my first mission of the day. I took a few hundred bucks and drove around town, stopping at a few different places and buying them out of their stock of beer and ice. Eventually, my Jetta was loaded down, and my tires were touching the wheel well.

After lugging everything into my apartment from the garage, I came to discover that my fridge was not big enough to handle what I had bought. So I decided to make all the bathtubs in my apartment into coolers. Each bathtub got beer and ice dumped into them. Based on the amount of beer, the party was going to be epic.

With the beer taken care of, I turned to my second mission of the day, games. I had the space in my apartment for games, but I did not have furniture designed for beer pong, flip cup, etc. I eventually figured out ways to repurpose the furniture I did have.

I put a large cupboard on its side to have a flip cup table. I had my dining table in one of the bedrooms for beer pong. Additionally, my large living room was transformed into a dance floor with colored lights in the overhead fixture. By six o'clock on the night of the party, my apartment was ready to go. I had even found red Solo cups for the games. My apartment looked and felt like a college house. Now it was a matter of who would show up, and if they would embrace U.S. college life.

My fear of no one showing up quickly vanished. First, my close friends arrived, Sarah and Natalie, other UN people, a few Nordic diplomats, and Vuk. The party slowly started to build, and by eight o'clock my large apartment was getting full.

As people arrived, I would greet them, and they told me it was difficult to find parking. New arrivals also started telling me my neighbors were helping my guests.

I had been a little nervous about what my neighbors would think of a huge party, but it seemed like they were embracing it. Maybe they were happy that in sad times people were still celebrating something. The neighbors sent their kids out to the street to walk the guests up to my apartment. The kids crewed the elevator to take people to the right floor. I even had a guest ask me if I had paid the kids to help out. I had not paid them, but I knew I would be buying them all candy very soon.

By 10 p.m. the party had transformed into a raging "college party" success. College Shawn would have been very proud of diplomat Shawn.

I think he would have been most proud because I was with what I knew to be the most wonderful woman at the party. When Amal arrived, she greeted me with her magic smile that caused her eyes to sparkle. She had come with a few of her friends, and I told them all that my house was their house tonight and to enjoy themselves. As I walked her friends from the front door into the party, Amal gave me a look that was more powerful than words. I guess I had impressed her.

Throughout the party, I was hanging with Amal and had the opportunity to meet some of her friends. Her friends all thought the party was great. They kept on commenting how they felt like they were living in a U.S. movie.

In each room of my apartment, grown adults were throwing ping-pong balls, flipping empty cups on a table, and yelling at the person next to them when they failed to flip it on the first attempt. People were screaming in excitement and frustration when the ping-pong ball did not land in the beer. It was a true madhouse with beer being slopped and empty cans just thrown on the floor, which made me wish that I had gotten some extra trash cans. For some reason, I always forget parties generate trash.

From time to time I would leave Amal and do a lap around the house, making sure beer was still in the bathtubs and that everyone was having a good time. As I made my laps, I realized that I didn't even know everyone who was there. There were dozens of guests I had not met before, and each of them was finding their place to play games or chat with others. It felt like every Western diplomat and UN worker had come to my apartment. I remember thinking I should have had a party earlier as it would have made meeting people much more manageable.

By 11 p.m., the UN workers had taken over the flip cup table. The military guys from the different embassies had taken over the beer pong table. The Eastern Europeans had taken over my kitchen with a bottle of vodka. The Nordic diplomats were on the dance floor, and all my balconies were full of people smoking cigarettes.

Deputy chiefs of other Embassies sipped beers on the balcony. People in their twenties chatted with people in their sixties. Cheers were going up when a beer pong ball dropped in a red Solo cup. Screams erupted when one flip cup team flipped and drank faster than the other.

This party raged until way past midnight as the different groups rotated games and eventually started to mingle. Everyone was now speaking the same language of drunken laughter and excitement. I was full of joy as I walked around playing host.

Eventually, I knew it was coming to an end when security personnel from Embassies vomited in my kitchen sink. Slowly, groups of people started to leave, and I found myself on the balcony smoking and sipping a beer. As the party began to thin out, Amal's friends came and thanked me for having them. This is when Amal leaned over and whispered in my ear that she was staying. Suddenly I had butterflies in my stomach, and I wished that I was not as drunk as I was afraid I was.

After Amal's friends departed, we sat together on the balcony with the last of the guests. We smoked and laughed with the last of the drunks until the early morning hours. Finally, it was just the two of us.

I walked through the house to make sure no one had passed out under a table, and I locked the front door. With that, we both retreated to the bedroom.

There's a poem by Khalil Gibran that reads: "Live a true love story and tell no one, live happily and tell no one, people ruin beautiful things."

The following day, when we both woke up in my apartment, the light was streaming through the open windows. Fresh air lapped at us in bed, waking me from my sleep. I had never seen Amal in the morning light. She was beautifully tucked into the white sheets. I thought that she was tucked between clouds in the sky that only rained dreams of hope. That morning all I hoped for was more days in my future when I could wake up next to her.

Eventually, she woke from the breeze and opened her eyes. We just laid there together in clouds of hope. We talked, smiled, and kissed one another. We opened our eyes and hearts to each other that morning, and we did not want to ever leave that room.

Never leaving that room wasn't a choice. The outside world eventually came calling, and it was time for Amal to head home. I got up and opened the bedroom door. The smell of spilled beer and cigarettes came rushing in. I quickly shut the door, and we decided not to venture out for a little longer.

The time finally came when she had to depart. We both put ourselves together and opened back up the bedroom door to reveal a trashed apartment. I had forgotten how messed up places got after a raging college party.

Amal asked me if she should stay and help clean, but I told her I could handle it. With that, I tiptoed through the filth to the kitchen to grab a broom. With the broom in hand, I swept a path from the bedroom to the front door so Amal could leave.

At the front door, I told Amal how wonderful of a time I had with her. She told me that she had a wonderful time as well. We smiled and embraced at the front door and kissed. I could have stood in that door for hours making out with her that morning, but the smell of cigarettes and stale beer meant we only paused there for a few minutes before she departed. It was not as romantic of a goodbye as I would have liked.

After shutting the front door and turning around, I suddenly felt extraordinarily hungover, and the smell of the trashed house was not making it better. I did one lap around my apartment and saw what I already knew to be true. My apartment was trashed, and everywhere there were empty beer cans, broken glasses, and cracked red Solo cups. My entire place smelled of cigarettes, and glasses full of cigarette butts covered all of my tables and countertops.

The kitchen smelled like vomit from the sink. In the beer pong room, there were footprints six feet up on the white walls. I am still not sure how that happened. To say the least, if you were to judge a party based on the mess it produced, this party was a massive success.

Even though the party was a success, I was not in the mood to launch a "mission successful cleanup." Instead, I started with a shower and drank some more water. Then I realized there was another option.

Since arriving in Damascus, I'd hired someone to clean my apartment and do my laundry twice a week. The two people I had hired were from Sri Lanka and were already working for another person at the Embassy.

I know other people who throw parties schedule their cleaners to come the morning after. I instantly regretted not planning because if they would have come early, the whole place could've been clean. I could have slept in and woken up to an apartment that never looked like a raging party had taken place.

Standing in the shower trying to wash the hangover off of me, I decided that even if the cleaners were not coming today, I would not do anything. I did not want to waste a day off of work cleaning. Instead, while I was still drying off from the shower, I called one of the cleaners and told them to come Sunday morning to perform a deep clean on my apartment. Luckily for me, they said it would not be a problem. With that, I put on some clothes and left my apartment to get some greasy hangover food.

The next day before I left to work, the cleaners arrived at my apartment. When I opened the door to let them in, they were shocked by what they saw. I had told them they would be cleaning up after my party, but I don't think they expected cleaning up after a college party. I am sure they were asking themselves, "What the F has this American been doing?"

I kind of felt bad leaving the cleanup to them, but I handed them each triple their usual fee to make up for it. When I gave them crisp, clean U.S. bills, they smiled and said they would always be happy to clean for me after a party.

Chapter 26

GF

AMAL WAS MY GIRLFRIEND AFTER THE COLLEGE PARTY. Being at the party together made it clear to my friends and hers that we were a couple. I guess the party was like our official red carpet movie walk when tabloids would declare us an "official couple." The testing of the relationship waters was over, and now we both plunged headlong into one another.

As our relationship transitioned, some of the walls that stood between us crumbled. Amal let me into her inner courtyard. She allowed me to walk in her secret garden. In that fictional garden, we strolled with one another, holding hands and talking. We did not just talk about superficial things like the weather. Rather, she told me how her garden grew. Where all the seeds came from. What each flower and petal meant to her. How each one had to be watered a different amount to make them grow. Amal allowed me to understand how she became so lovely.

Our secret garden conversations did not take place in a garden, though. They did not take place over the phone or in my apartment with the third wheel. We had them sitting in my car on the street somewhere in Damascus.

I began to get to know her mom and dad through long, in-depth conversations. I got to know her sister through those same conversations. We were both peeling back our outer layers. On the surface, she was a middle-class Syrian woman, but there was so much more to her.

Like many parts of the world, Syria is not a homogenous society. Instead, it comprises a mix of people with different religions, origins, customs, and beliefs. Amal's family was from one of the religious minorities of Syria and the region. Amal came from a Druze family.

Druze are people that practice a monotheistic religion that incorporates religious beliefs from Islam, Judaism, and Christianity. It is also influenced by Greek philosophy and Hinduism. I did not know any of that at the time because Amal did not talk about the Druze religion. She just told me that her family origins are Druze, but she and her immediate family did not practice the religion. She could have also not told me anything because Druze's religious practices and beliefs are not shared with outsiders.

She did share that unlike most Druze in Syria, who come from the area around the "Druze Mountian," in Arabic, "Jibal al Durz," her family was from a Druze village in the Golan Heights. Her mom and dad, with their parents, had fled to Damascus just before the outbreak of the Six-Day War in June 1967. Since that war, none of her family members, mom, dad, grandmothers, or grandfathers, had ever been back to the village they grew up in.

Sitting in my car, we wondered if the Syrian uprising would

eventually mean she and her family would be forced to move again.

The idea of moving away from Damascus and leaving Syria seemed to be on everyone's mind in late 2011. If you were Syrian, whether pro or against the regime, you were looking for a way out.

It was even more critical for young men because most, I think, did not want to be forced into the Syrian military. Syrian men were required to complete at least two years of military service. However, there were ways to delay their service, like going to university. Also, if you were rich and had the right connections, you might be able to buy or bribe your way out of the service. By the end of 2011, the regime's military needed bodies, and avoiding military service was becoming next to impossible.

At the Embassy, we had to deal with this issue regularly because Syrian-American men were arriving at Damascus International Airport and detained. These Syrian-Americans were returning to Syria to check on loved ones or attend a parent's funeral.

We would hear about their detention from their U.S. side of the family. They would call us at the Embassy to tell us they were detained and ordered to complete their Syrian military service. These people had skipped out years earlier on their military service by moving to the U.S. or through some other exception. Now, the regime was going to force them to join their side or try and extract money from them to let them leave.

As a woman, Amal did not have to worry about military conscription, which is lucky because she had no love for the military.

She told me how all Syrians, even girls, had to fire a gun in school. She said she was so scared and hated it.

Even though Amal and her female friends did not have to worry about military service, many wanted out of Syria. After meeting some of her friends, it became clear they were looking for a way out of Syria. They were all college graduates, and they seemed to think doing a master's program abroad was a possible path out. I even helped a few of them with their master's applications. I guess even with dyslexia, I could help a little.

At this point in Damascus, not all of the Syrians who told me they wanted to leave desired to leave because of violence. Every day the Syrian black market rate for U.S. dollars increased as the Syrian pound lost value. Prices of goods were going up, but wages for Syrians were not. Many private companies were prospering before the uprising, but now they were laying people off. It became clear to young, educated Syrians that if they could find work outside of Syria, they should take it.

However, sitting in my car with Amal under the dim street lights of the city, she told me she was not going to leave. Her family was all in Damascus. Her dad was still getting a government pension and had not worked for years. Her mother was still working at a school in Damascus. For Amal, her home was Damascus because her family was there.

She was finding it extremely difficult to witness Syria falling apart. It had been stable for her entire life. Of course, there had been wars with Israel. There had been assassinations and bombings in the past. There had been sanctions before and economic hardships. However, Amal stressed this time was different. Her country was being divided and torn apart from the inside.

When we broached the subject of the revolution, of the civil war, Amal's eyes would water up and tears would flow. It was a subject that could and did only bring sadness into her life.

I lived the revolution for months at work, I found it tragic, and it kept me up at night, but since my loved ones, my family and friends, were safe in the United States, it did not affect me the same way it did for people who had loved ones in Syria.

Now, having someone I now loved, even though I had not told her yet, who was directly impacted by the events in Syria changed me. I wanted Syria to be peaceful. I wanted Amal to be happy and safe.

Sitting there doing my sitreps, adding up bodies, writing sad tales of attacks and failed plans for peace, I would now start crying. I would be sitting at my desk and tears would fall on my keyboard because very bad things impacted a person I loved.

Even though it made me sad, I still compiled the sitreps and went to meetings to somehow communicate to the U.S. government what was happening—to try and give them the feeling on the ground. I tried to convey that things were getting worse, peaceful diplomatic solutions were failing, and the violence was real. A sense of inevitability was spreading.

By November 27, the Arab League was over its peace plans and joined the West by sanctioning Syria. Syria was indeed now an outcast of the diplomatic world—they were now just hanging out with the likes of North Korea and Iran.

The sanctions were having an impact on Syrian currency and jobs. Syrians and the regime were all suffering. However, the sanctions did not seem to bring the regime any closer to collapsing or surrendering.

More people were defecting from the Syrian Army and joining the Free Syrian Army. More people were being displaced internally as city neighborhoods and villages became battlegrounds. Deaths rose and rose.

Eventually, by December 1, the UN reported a death toll of 4,000 due to the revolution. It was also on December 1, 2011, that the UN stated it was "characterizing it as a civil war."

I was doing my duty of sending my reports back to Washington, hoping that they would help policymakers understand that dramatic actions needed to be taken to avoid an all-out war. More sanctions and diplomatically isolating the regime was not a path to peace.

From Damascus, I wanted to yell at the capital-based decision-makers sitting in meeting rooms thousands of miles away from Syria to get off their asses and do something. Bring everyone to the table. Figure out a path to peace.

Maybe capital-based decision-makers thought an unstable Syria was good because it weakened an ally of Iran. Perhaps they saw polling that said their citizens did not want tax dollars spent in the Middle East. Maybe they thought it would not help them win reelection. I didn't know.

I only knew that being in Syria and seeing firsthand what was happening made me mad because the world was not working together to figure out an amicable solution. What was the UN doing? Who was vetoing actions by the Security Council? How was the rest of the world going to watch as a country tore itself apart? These were questions I asked myself daily.

I kept on yelling through the words I wrote in cables. I high-lighted the problems, the deaths, the violence, the lack of justice. I hoped somehow my small voice would bounce around the echo chambers of government until it was amplified to the halls of power.

But sitting in the car after work with Amal, my voice felt weak. There were no reassuring words I could offer her. I could not tell her not to worry about her family, her city, or her country.

Sometimes we wouldn't speak, we would just hold one an-other and find comfort in being close. Somehow holding her hand or placing my head on her lap offered us both some odd sense of stability and comfort while sitting in a car in the capital of a country falling apart.

CHAPTER 27

Meet the Family

THE DAY THE UN SAID THERE WAS A CIVIL WAR IN SYRIA did not mean there was a formal declaration of war. It was not like World War II when there was a definitive start to war like the bombing of Pearl Harbor or the invasion of Poland. There was no absolute point marking the transition between peace, revolution, and war.

In the beginning, peaceful protesters were calling for reforms. Then protestors started asking for the downfall of the regime. Protesters became opposition members, and those opposition members slowly started to include defectors from the Syrian military.

To put it simply, Syria transitioned into a civil war because there were enough opposition members armed and fighting against the regime. Before, it was just the regime killing unarmed people. The armed opposition were members of the Free Syrian Army (FSA) or other armed opposition groups. It seemed like each week a new group formed with a new name and a new leader. However, just because new armed opposition groups were forming didn't mean those groups were powerful.

The two sides in the Syrian civil war were not equal. There were reports of twenty soldiers defecting here and another thirty defecting there. Having a few people defecting was not a clear division of the Syrian military. It was not like the U.S. Civil War when the South attempted to break away, U.S. Generals suddenly chose sides, and the country is divided.

Before the revolution, the Syrian military had over 300,000 people under arms and almost the same number as reservists. The big question was, how many soldiers would leave the regime and join the opposition? Would high-level commanders switch sides and bring their troops with them?

In late 2011, part of the opposition had militarized but in no way did they have the numbers or equipment to win an overall military victory over the Assad Regime. The opposition did not have the power to ride into central Damascus and march on the regime's headquarters and government buildings.

The two sides in the Syrian civil war were lopsided. The regime had the majority of the guns, all of the planes, almost all of the tanks, all of the helicopters, the majority of the artillery, and more soldiers.

By late 2011, the armed opposition still hoped thousands upon thousands of soldiers would switch sides. I think capitals also wished the Syrian military would splinter. They hoped some great general would emerge from the many armed opposition groups that could bring them all together under one leadership structure. Maybe by calling it a civil war, policymakers were trying to make their dream of a clearly defined, two-sided conflict a reality.

The label of "civil war" might have influenced policymakers or briefings at the UN, but it was just another day in Damascus. The city was still running. People who had jobs still went to work, and people still sat in cafes drinking strong coffee, smoking, and playing backgammon. I still had to do the sitrep, and protests were still happening, but mostly now near Homs and Hama.

December 2 was the "Friday of the Syrian Buffer Zone." People around Syria again went to the streets. They called for a safe zone along its border with Turkey. The opposition was now openly asking for outside support in the civil war. They were asking for protection because their forces could not do it. They needed outside forces, especially Turkey, to create a buffer zone.

As the opposition called for a buffer zone, I was trying to remove all buffers in the relationship between Amal and me. It was time for me to meet her family.

Amal talked to me about her family all of the time. I formed a picture in my head of who they were based on our conversations, so I was excited when she asked me if I wanted to meet her sister, Zahar. I knew it was a big deal to introduce me to her sister; she was one of the closest people to Amal.

We decided to meet at a small restaurant/bar in the center of town. It would kind of be like a double date with Zahar and her boyfriend, Abel. It would not be an "interrogate Shawn night" to find out if I was suitable for Amal. However, I was ready if Zahar wanted to start asking hard questions.

When I walked into the restaurant, I scanned the room, looking for the three of them. After a glance around, I saw Amal, and it was pretty clear who her sister was. I was shocked because

Amal and Zahar looked so much alike. They both had the same face and body type and some of the same facial expressions.

Before I sat down at the table, I kissed Amal on the cheek and shook hands with Zahar and Abdel. As I shook Zahar's hand, I was happy to hear Amal introduce me as her boyfriend.

I was nervous as I sat down at the table with them. I wondered if they would pepper me with questions or if there would be awkward conversations. I wanted so badly to make an excellent first impression.

To help us get over the nerves of first encounters, we ordered a round of drinks, and after a few minutes of sipping on them, I started to ask Zahar about herself.

She was happy to tell me all about her life as a pastry chef. Additionally, Abdel told me about his life as a professional chef. It seemed like Amal and Zahar had taken very different paths— one in an office and one in a kitchen.

I also found out Abdel was a Palestinian-Syrian. That might not sound important, but it was to me. Palestinians in most of the Arab world are not viewed in a positive light by other Arabs. Mostly they are treated as second-class citizens, or not even as citizens. They can live in Arab countries for generations but never become part of society. They are stateless and, in many places, live on the fringes of society.

Additionally, he was not Druze! This meant that Amal's parents were very progressive because they accepted a non-Druze to be with their daughter. Abdel's background gave me hope. If Amal's parents could accept him, a Palestinian non-Druze, maybe they would also accept me, an American.

After we all got to know a little about each other, I told funny stories and heard funny stories about Amal's childhood from Zahar. Amal, throughout the evening, did not say much, but she smiled as her sister and I talked.

I could tell by Zahar's questions that Amal had already told her a lot about me. I guess Amal was sitting back and letting Zahar play the role of a good older sister by making sure I was not an ass. By the end of the evening, Amal's smile told me, "Thanks for confirming to my sister that you are what I told her you are—a good person."

I had a wonderful evening with the three of them that night, and I hoped we could do it again soon. At the end of the night, I kissed Amal's cheek goodbye and waved to Zahar and Abdel as we all headed off in different directions.

By this point in early December, Amal and I had become each other's best friends in Syria. If we did not see one another, then we were calling each other every night. I had a physical need to hear her voice. Her voice was some kind of comforting drug to me. When I heard her or when I saw her in person, the world around me brightened.

However, even if she brightened my day, the darkness around us cast a shadow on our relationship. At this point, I likely lost a measure of professionalism needed in my line of work. Firstly, I stayed up too late talking to Amal and was tired when I got to the office in the morning. But more importantly, I now had a much stronger emotional tie to Syria because of Amal. I was not unbiased when trying to look at the situation. I still reported the facts as they were on the ground, but the tone of those facts had my emotions sprinkled in. I was not merely looking at things from the interests of the United States; I was looking at my interest in Syria, which was Amal.

I wanted peace. I wanted a solution. I wanted Amal to be happy. I did not care about weakening Iran's influence or the downfall of the regime and a democratic Syria. I just wanted everyone to sit down and stop fighting. We could figure the rest out later. I wanted to scream, "How the hell do humans get to a point when the only answer is violence!"

Even if I screamed, no one was listening. People only heard the beating of the war drums. The calls to arms. Peace was not loud enough to be heard over the roar of cannons.

Instead, Amal and I both agreed over messages, "Well, thank God there is alcohol with the situation getting more complicated... Getting drunk and forgetting is, unfortunately, the best thing to be done right now."

CHAPTER 28

Americans Need to Know

I HAD NEVER BEEN TOTALLY OPEN WITH MY FAMILY about my past relationships and tended to avoid conversations involving feelings, even when pressed by my mom. I guess it was no surprise that I only made vague references to Amal and life in Damascus when I talked to or emailed family or friends.

In addition to avoiding my personal life, I also did not discuss work with my family or friends. They did not need to know about my meetings on street corners or the death count. Instead, I always said the same line to everyone who asked about my work—I would just say, "It is very interesting."

My family eventually understood that "interesting" just stood for "stop asking me about work." Also, I am sure my calls and emails with them were not wholly private in Syria, so I figured I would stay away from any work-related subjects.

In addition to saying work was interesting, my emails home had another common thread. I used the word "depressing" a lot. By early December, I was telling people back home, "Daily, it seems less and less likely that peace and love will come to Syria any time soon."

Even though I was not writing home to my family and friends about precisely what was going on in Syria, I was sending cables with the hope the U.S. government would understand and take action. However, I was not naive enough to believe that if the U.S. government knew something terrible was happening it would take action.

The U.S. is run by politicians who usually take action only when the people, U.S. citizens, demand that action occur. Additionally, the U.S. government is not the driver that convinces citizens when action should and should not take place.

The White House or the State Department could hold press briefings, and government spokespeople could show videos and satellite images of Syria's slide into chaos. At the Embassy, Ambassador Ford could write up some social media posts. But in the end, the U.S. government could not produce good content.

The government is not known for its quality media output. Thus, if the U.S. government wants to connect to the American people, it needs the help of the private sector.

If the government wanted to take action in Syria, if it was going to spend millions or billions of dollars supporting the opposition, if U.S. troops were going to be on the ground, then the U.S. people needed to understand what was happening. To get the American people that information, there needed to be U.S. or Western media on the ground in Syria to broadcast the information back to the American people.

However, no Western journalists were being allowed into Syria by the regime. The regime was doing its best to control the media story by publicizing their truths and calling other facts lies. I have no doubt that the regime understood the critical role of controlling the media narrative.

The Assad Regime had been controlling the narrative for years through the arrest and intimidation of journalists. It also had built a state media system to control the media story to its citizens, but now technology was weakening their control. Syrians with cell phone cameras captured videos, pictures, and sounds that were making their way through Syria and eventually to the West.

I think it's excellent when citizens become journalists and document what is happening. However, although a ten-second video or a good photo might make people pause in shock when it depicts a dead child buried in rubble or when a child turns white after a gas attack, those images alone can't move society. People need stories to understand what is happening. Stories must tell us why the child was buried in the rubble and what happened to the child with blue lips and a white face. To tell a good story, there needed to be professional storytellers. I think those professional storytellers are called journalists.

For months, the Western media ran stories with the photos and videos taken in Syria by Syrians. Even though the journalists were not in Syria, they were trying to tell Syrian stories. The journalists were sitting in Beirut, Lebanon, a two-hour drive from Damascus, on rooftops with minarets in the background of their TV interviews to try and show their U.S. audience they were close to the action. For the average American, reporting from Beirut might as well have been reporting from Homs. It seemed like the Western media was there on the ground and had the scoop.

People in the U.S. were starting to hear the tragic stories coming from Syria. The media was doing its job of reporting the truth. Professionals were transforming short video clips and pictures from citizen journalists in Syria into digestible narratives for the U.S. population. The regime might have been controlling journalists in Syria, but it was losing the global media battle.

In an attempt to get the regime's side of the truth out to the world, the regime somehow decided to bring in one of the top U.S. journalists. They agreed that if this person could show their side of the story, they could drown out the other Western journalists in Beirut or the other few who had snuck into Syria. The famous journalist the regime decided to bring in was none other than Barbara Walters.

Not only would Barbara Walters be coming to Damascus, she was also going to interview Assad. It would be the first interview Assad would give since the uprising started ten months before. In addition to Barbara, another ABC journalist, Alexander Marquardt, arrived a few days before her.

At the Embassy, we were not aware ABC was planning a trip. After the trip had been arranged and the visas issued by the regime, we got an email from ABC saying they were coming and asked to meet with someone at the Embassy.

When I heard they were coming, I was excited that a major U.S. TV network would be in Syria to report on the uprising. I oddly hoped that Barbara would be able to galvanize the American people to demand action from their elected officials. I hoped that somehow her star power would rally the masses. Now I just wondered what role I could play—it turned out, a minor one.

ABC wanted a "backgrounder," and I was told to provide this to Alexander Marquardt. I had never given a "backgrounder" to a journalist, so I asked what I should do. I was told Marquardt was not going to interview me, he was not going to quote me, instead I was to help him understand the Syrian uprising and the current state of affairs.

After a few emails with Marquardt, we had decided on a date and time to meet. I also understood I was not just meeting with Marquardt. The regime, I was sure, told Marquardt he was free to go where he wanted when he wanted and talk to whoever he wanted. The regime was going to say it had nothing to hide, but they would watch him exceptionally closely. They would have "minders" with him to ensure they understood who he talked to and what he saw.

I met Marquardt at a cafe in Damascus, and I am sure I was in full view of his minders. I did not mind if they saw me. What I was talking to him about was no secret in Syria, and in many ways, he did not even need the briefing as he was quite knowledgeable.

However, one thing he did say shocked me. He told me that he could travel freely outside of Damascus. Assad later echoed this during his interview with Walters, which Marquardt sat in on. If Marquardt was allowed to travel outside of Damascus, he would be even freer than me.

I encouraged him to get out of the capital because central Damascus was not where the revolution was taking place. I wanted him to go out and see for himself what citizen journalists captured on their cell phones. I wanted him to see the regime's violence and tell that story to the American people. I figured that the American people would see the need to do more than enact a few sanctions after a professional storyteller told them Syria's story.

ABC later reported, after Marquardt and Walters left Syria, that President Assad claimed he would allow an ABC News reporter to travel anywhere. Still, in reality, when Marquardt went out, he found his movements closely watched and restricted by both uniformed and plainclothes security officers. The regime was not letting him see and tell the real story as he wanted to.

A few days after I sat down with Marquardt, the star of the show came to town. When Barbara Walters arrived in Damascus, a few of us from the Embassy met with her at the Ambassador's stately house, with its gardens, high walls, and grand rooms.

Sitting there talking to her, I was kind of jealous that she would have a chance to question Assad. I wanted to question him to understand why he had led Syria down a path of destruction. I wanted to slap him in the face and say, "Wake up and do something to stop the violence. Stop the country you say you love from becoming the next killing field in the history books." I would never get the chance to ask him these questions. But everyone at the Embassy that day encouraged Barabara to ask hard questions.

After we met with Barabara, I wished her the best. As her car left, I stood there at the front door of the Ambassador's mansion, hoping she would be able to get a story from Assad. A story the American people and the world could understand. A story that would pull at their heartstrings, that would somehow push them to demand the U.S. take action.

I never got to meet Assad and for sure never got to slap him across the face. Instead, Barbara Walters and the ABC team got to go over to Assad's Presidential Palace and sit face to face with him. She got to ask him the questions, and I, like the rest of the world, had to wait a day for the interview to be broadcast to see how Assad would answer.

The same day Walters was interviewing Assad, December 6, we learned that Ford would return to Damascus. I guessed when the U.S. government knew Assad's name would be splashed across their citizens' TV screens, the administration wanted their Ambassador on the ground. State Department spokesman Mark Toner said in a statement on December 6, "We believe his presence in the country is among the most effective ways to send the message that the United States stands with the people of Syria."

It was clear from the messaging and the actions of top U.S. officials that the policy on Syria was ramping up. Walters's timing for an interview could not have been any better. The announcement of Ford's return to Syria came on the same day Secretary of State Hillary Clinton met in Geneva with Syrian exiles, members of the so-called Syrian National Council.

There, Clinton called for a "democratic transition," which "includes more than removing the Assad Regime." The U.S. and other countries in Europe, Turkey, and Jordan had called for the Assad Regime to step down after four decades in power. Now, through Walters's interview with Assad, maybe the world would see if stepping down was on the table. Was it still possible to achieve a peaceful political transition?

On December 7, 2011, Walters's interview with Assad aired in the U.S. I am not going to go into all of the questions and answers. The full transcript of the interview is online. The gist of the interview can be summed up in a few lines from Assad, who said, "We don't kill our people. No government in the world kills its people, unless it's led by a crazy person. For me, as president, I became president because of the public support. It's impossible for anyone—in this state, to give orders to kill people." When I listened to the interview and heard Assad's words, I was in shock.

I was counting and seeing the dead daily in my office. After ten months of the uprising, 4,000-plus people had been killed in Syria. A verbal denial could not cover the evidence of this violence and death by Assad.

Walters said after the interview that there was a disconnect between what Assad said and what was really going on in Syria. State Department Deputy Spokesperson Toner said, "Just from what happened or what took place in the interview, he appeared utterly disconnected with the reality that's going on in his country and the brutal repression that's being carried out against the Syrian people." He added, "It's either disconnection, disregard or, as he said, crazy. I don't know."

When I talked to a Syrian friend about the interview, he said, "He still surprises us every time... He is still successful at shocking us with the denial and the delusion."

I do not think Assad was crazy or disconnected. He knew what was going on and had chosen to tell bald-faced lies to the world. I don't think he cared if the world believed him. He wanted to give regime loyalists talking points. He needed them to be able to say, "I heard Assad say he was not responsible for the killings, and I believe him."

A few days later, the opposition again went to the streets on a Friday of protests. On December 9 the protests were labeled the Friday of "Dignity Strike." At least forty-one people were reported killed by the regime that day, according to members of the opposition.

After the interview, it was also time for Ford to come back because Syria was now on the nightly news in the U.S., and the world's only superpower needed their man back on the ground. Ford was back in town and, according to spokesman Toner, was going to "continue the work he was doing previously; namely, delivering the United States' message to the people of Syria; providing reliable reporting on the situation on the ground; and engaging with the full spectrum of Syrian society on how to end the bloodshed and achieve a peaceful political transition." The issue of Ford's safety, the reason he left in the first place, was not addressed by the State Department when announcing his return.

The French Ambassador had also arrived back in Damascus a few days before Ford. The capitals had sent their top people back to stir the pot.

I was happy to have Ford back because I knew he wouldn't merely sit there. He was going to push the situation away from war. I believe that the situation needed to be pushed because it was moving toward a tipping point. If it went over, it meant a long civil war was going to happen.

By early December, many people already thought a civil war was the only logical next step for Syria. I still had hope for some sort of resolution, some type of government reforms, peace talks, or maybe Assad would just leave and take asylum somewhere. I hoped for the best, but planned for the worst—that was my perspective in early December.

Part of my hope still came through spending time with Amal. During the evening, Amal would come over and we would sit on the balcony overlooking Damascus as the sun went down. Holding hands, I would look at her and see the beauty of a country represented in a person. That beauty inspired hope in me because who would purposely destroy such beauty?

CHAPTER 29

Pushing Policy

WHEN FORD RETURNED IT WAS EVIDENT that Embassy Damascus was no longer the driving force of U.S. policy. Ford's public statements and actions before were at the forefront of U.S. policy, but now DC had fully jumped on board and was steering the boat.

People might think the U.S. Ambassador is the top person when dealing with the country for which they are the Ambassador, but that's not the case. There are many layers between the Ambassador and the President of the United States. There are layers in the State Department in DC, and there are also layers at the National Security Council (NSC). These layers mean the people on the ground, the Ambassador included, get their information filtered through layers of bureaucracy before it reaches the primary decision-maker, the President of the United States.

Understanding how to navigate the layers is an important skill, but sitting at my desk every day in Damascus, the layers above me kept getting more and more crowded. If Syria was now the hot topic of the international community, everyone wanted a piece of the action.

My colleagues and I were still very motivated to get information to DC, but now not all news was coming from us. There seemed to be enough Syrian opposition outside of Syria talking to Washington that we were getting drowned out by other "experts" on Syria that knew what was going on while sitting in Paris or Istanbul.

The uprising had been occurring for ten months and shifted from calls for reforms to calls for the complete collapse of the regime and a replacement. Syrian opposition representatives, who all claimed to be the "true representatives of the Syrian people," gave speeches and held meetings in France, Spain, Turkey, London, etc. These groups of people, or even individuals, all had different plans and either claimed to have power in Syria or claimed to have the inside scoop. In many ways, the competition between Syrian opposition members was the biggest threat to the revolution. There was a competition between nations to be friends with Syrian dissidents abroad as every dissident claimed to be the leader behind the revolution. In and outside of Syria, the opposition and revolution was a shit show.

I did not concern myself with the people outside of Syria. I felt that these "outside forces" were dangerous and made up their truths to serve their means. I was on the ground in Syria and hoped to remain there instead of going to some safe European capital for meetings.

The other major change when Ford returned was security. I spent many hours upon his return shredding papers and making sure the Embassy was void of anything sensitive if we needed to make a quick exit.

Like any Embassy, we had carried out drills on what to do in case of an attack. Every week, the Marines tested the "duck and cover alarms," and I would sit at my desk wondering what I would do if we were attacked. Would I be able to make it out of the Embassy if a regime mob stormed it?

Like all U.S. Embassies and Consulates, there was an evacuation plan in place, but I also thought the plans sucked. We were in a building surrounded by regime forces. We were in a city controlled by the regime. We had a few armored cars and a wall around a small building. If the regime wanted to hurt us, kill us, or take us hostage, they could do so with little effort. So, the "plans" all sucked.

However, I was happy to be there because I believed the regime would not risk an all-out attack on the Embassy. That would undoubtedly bring the fury of the U.S. government. However, as our Secretary of State met with opposition figures outside of Syria, I started to wonder if the regime would change its tune and think, "They are already against us. Let's get some hostages like in Iran."

If a mob showed up and broke down the doors, what would happen to us? Because there was no good plan, I thought I would come up with one for myself. We had a safe room, but safe rooms are not safe forever, and if the mob had the time, they would eventually get into the Embassy. I knew I needed to figure out how to get out of the Embassy if we were overrun.

Next to my desk, I had a change of clothes—jeans, a white shirt, and a leather jacket. I thought of it as my Shabiha outfit. If a mob showed up, I figured I would put on my Syrian mafia outfit and wait for them to come into the Embassy. Right before I thought they were going to break down the door, I was going to grab Ambassador Ford and punch him in the face. When the mob entered, I would announce to them while holding the bloody Ambassador, "Don't worry, guys, I already got him," as I made it through the back door.

Maybe they would somehow believe I was on their side, and I could join the mob, leave the Embassy, and slip away into the Damascus streets. Like I said before, it was a bad plan, but at least I had a plan. I did not want to sit in a safe room waiting for the mob to come and get me. I once even jokingly told Ambassador Ford my plan, but he did not think highly of it.

I also came up with a second plan of escape from Syria if I was outside the Embassy when it was overrun. If shit went down, I figured I would have to find a way out of Syria and not just wait in my apartment. My "get out of Syria plan" was a little better than my "escape from the Embassy" plan.

It just so happened that when I bought my Jetta, there were old Jordanian diplomatic plates in the trunk. I guessed that years ago a U.S. diplomat in Jordan must've owned my car. So, I planned to take off my Syrian diplomatic plates, which let people know I was from the U.S. Embassy, and switch them to Jordanian diplomatic plates. That was step one.

Step two was going to other Embassies in Syria to hide. I am sure I could have gone to the Canadians, Brits, or other Western countries for safety. However, I figured if the U.S. was going to get attacked, I would not be safe at Western Embassies. I needed to find an embassy a little more eastern. I had become good friends with two of the three diplomats at the Serbian Embassy in Damascus. For the most part, Syrians just considered the Serbians as Russians, which they were not, but for my escape plans, it was good enough. Pro-regime Syrians loved the Russians, so I figured if all went to hell and I needed a place to hide, I would beg the Serbians to take me in.

Even though my BS plans made me feel better, I was powerless. I am sure that if the regime decided to, they could have rolled me up any time they wanted. Having plans is sometimes the only mental safety available to make people still feel in control. In reality, I had lost control a long time ago in Syria.

The only thing that seemed to have some semblance of stability, something that I could control, was my relationship with Amal. Neither of us were making plans to run away from our relationship. Instead, as the world around us spiraled out of control, each night we found comfort in each other.

Nightly meetings or long phone calls helped us both believe that there was no escaping the way we felt about one another. Although we never brought up our future plans, both of us still felt there was a future for us.

Like an old Arabic poem says, "I love looking at the moon when it's still a crescent because I love everything that has a future." Amal was my crescent moon. I could not see a future for Syria, but I saw a future for us.

CHAPTER 30

Breaking Down

AT THE END OF NOVEMBER, I had started to make plans for my first break from Syria. My first rest and relaxation trip, a R&R. As part of those plans, I talked to my mom, who was desperate to see me, and by early December, my family and I had agreed to meet in Europe for Christmas.

My family has terrific Dutch friends, who I consider my European family, and we had all shared Christmas before, so we decided to spend the holidays with them in Holland. We would have a big Dutch Christmas.

My family was excited to see me, and I was excited to see them. I wanted a break from Syria more than anything else. Physically and emotionally, I was drained. Every day the death count took something out of me. Whatever it took from me made it more difficult to smile. It became harder for me to laugh and easier to cry.

All day, every day, I thought, read, saw, and lived the tragedy of collapse. The only break from the madness was when Amal and I spent time together. We would stare at one another in a dimly lit bar, in my car under a street light, or in my apartment, and we would lose ourselves in stupid stories and daydreams.

She would tell me how her cat was a mean and vicious ruler of her family's apartment. She would tell me how her cat would bite her for no reason and always watch her, waiting to attack. We talked about future trips we would take together. We dreamt of visiting the beach on the Syrian coast and sipping drinks in the sun.

The mental breaks with Amal never lasted long enough, and when they ended, I found myself back in the maelstrom of a revolution.

I am sure that many Syrians were doing what we were—trying to escape reality by daydreaming. However, unlike almost every Syrian, I could make those dreams a reality.

I had a U.S. diplomatic passport. I could leave Syria. There were still a few commercial flights coming into Damascus, and if I wanted to, I could have gone to the airport, boarded a plane, and left. In a few hours, I could be sitting in a safe, stable, and nice place. I could be on the beach, in the sun, and sipping a cold drink if I wanted. However, unlike my dream, Amal's life as a Syrian was limited by reality.

I was privileged to be able to escape the evil of the regime. Even if Syrians had the funds to buy a ticket, they didn't have a visa to another country. Most Syrians were stuck, and many of them would never leave. By December 12, the UN estimated 5,000 people had died in Syria since the uprising started. Those 5,000 would never get a chance to live their daydreams, and the living were left wondering if their dreams would ever become a reality.

I would sit with Amal's Syrian friends, listen to stories of people losing their jobs, and wonder if they would find anything else. I would listen to Syrians discuss plans to leave Syria. I would hear stories of Amal's friends vanishing. I would hear diplomats complain that war was coming or that it was already here. I would listen to stories and more stories, all of them sad. How could I be planning a relaxing getaway with my family with this going on?

At the time, I didn't realize how much it all was affecting me. Only looking back years later can I truly understand the impact the sadness had on me. The State Department's training did not prepare me for this. I was not ready to be a diplomat in a revolution. I was definitely not prepared to be a diplomat in a war.

At this point, I could not disconnect myself from Syria. I was in a relationship with Syria. I was in love with Syria. But it was not a good relationship. It was a tragic, abusive relationship built on shared sadness and pain.

My relationship with Amal mirrored my relationship with Syria. However, when it was just the two of us, we tried to live in the blissful dreamland of our newfound love. Like many relationships, there are different phases. Amal and I first went through the "get to know you phase." Then came the "I like you" phase. Then we got to know one another on a deeper level. By December, we were onto the word "Habibiti" or "Habibi."

"Habibiti" in Arabic means "my love." This phrase is used in the Middle East by many people. It can be used by mothers and fathers when referring to their kids. It is used between long-time friends. It is said in almost every Arabic romantic song ever written and sung. It is also used between a boyfriend and girlfriend.

This woman I met in the uprising had become my Habibiti. Using Habibiti is different than saying, "I love you." Instead, it might be the step right before it happens. She had become "my love" in a very short period of time.

This relationship had not developed over years or months. It was a relationship counted in weeks. Still, it didn't feel rushed. We both felt like it was meant to be. We both fell headlong into it.

We were two people from different cultures and backgrounds. We were brought together in an uprising. Our relationship was built in a dark place because we both wanted some light.

Things in Damascus were getting dark in actuality. Not in my neighborhood because I was close to the regime's headquarters, but in many areas of Damascus, power cuts started to become the norm. I would call Amal after work, and she would be sitting in the dark of her family's apartment. While power cuts had happened in Damascus previously, they weren't typical. Now, their frequency and length were increasing.

Driving Amal home, close to the mountains and toward Barzeh, streets were empty at night, and many neighborhoods we passed through were suffering power cuts. It seemed like people in the city had closed their doors early. Fewer cars moved on the roads, and the city was eerily quiet.

During the day, the city felt alive but unwell. People were out and about. People who had jobs still went to work. Places were open but not crowded.

Syrians were using their money wisely. Getting a hookah and playing backgammon was still cheap, and you could sit there all day in a cafe with smoke and a game board. People were making their money last as best they could. Stores that had Western products when I arrived no longer carried them. Sanction and war were having an impact. The Syrian pound was not performing, and everyone was happy to take my dollars when I went out.

The economic collapse also changed the way I socialized. Apartments and houses had become the popular hangout places because most Syrians did not have extra cash to spend at bars. Amal and I were spending more time in mixed groups of friends—Syrians and foreigners. I had Amal and her girlfriends over to my apartment, and I would play the good host and provide drinks for everyone.

Driving Amal home after one such gathering, Amal gave me a photo. In Damascus, I did not have a smartphone. I only had a little Nokia. I could not just look at a picture of Amal on my iPhone. So, Amal gave me an old passport photo of herself. It was not a good photo like most passport photos, but it meant the world to me. I placed it in my wallet like people from my father's generation.

This gift of a simple passport photo meant so much to me; it could go with me wherever I went. If I left Syria, Amal was coming with me in some way.

It was especially nice to have a picture of Amal because I wanted to show my parents what she looked like when I saw them. Amal knew by early December that I would see my family for Christmas in Europe, and I was very excited to tell my family about Amal.

In conversations with my parents and brothers, I had shared little with them about Amal. I figured it was better to tell them I was in love when I saw them in person. As Christmas got closer,

I got more excited for a break and more excited to tell my family about the woman I had met.

However, even as I prepared for vacation, the Syrian uprising was raging. On December 16, the opposition called for a "Friday of the Arab League is Killing Us." It seemed like people wanted outside support to find a way for peace to come to Syria. Hope was on life support, and at least twenty-two people died that Friday.

CHAPTER 31
Don't Come Back

THE TIME OF MY VACATION WAS APPROACHING, and I was getting excited to see my family. I was still doing the daily sitrep and still trying to hear from the Syrian people. I figured my R&R would be an excellent two-week break, and I would be returning to continue my mission. However, a few days before I was scheduled to leave, I got called into the Ambassador's office.

It was not a strange thing for me to get called in to talk to Ford. There were so few of us left that we all interacted with him on a daily basis.

As I walked to the Ambassador's office, I wondered what questions he had about the day's sitrep. But when I got to his office, he did not have any questions. He and Clayton were standing there with serious faces. Something else was up.

"Enjoy your R&R," Ford began. Then he added, "You will not be coming back to Damascus."

I stood there. I am sure I had a blank expression on my face. I did not want to hear those words.

Before I could say anything, he continued, "You cannot tell

anyone that you're not coming back from R&R."

I only remember asking one question to the Ambassador. "Well, what will I do after Europe?"

"We will figure that out once you are in Europe," he responded. "Someone will reach out to you while you are there."

That was it. There was no discussion or conversation. Just a quick exchange and I walked out of his office. I was in shock. Normally I would have had a lot more questions for him and Clayton. Instead, I went back to my desk and sat there staring at one of my computer screens.

From my first day in Syria, I had known I could be pulled out at any time. I should have been mentally prepared for my departure. I should have known this was going to happen. There was no way the Embassy could remain open if the civil war continued to spiral out of control.

Sitting at my desk, the shock slowly faded, and my mind started to grasp what this meant. First, if I was leaving that meant and the Embassy would be closing very soon. This means DC must have decided to ramp up pressure on the regime. Things were going to be getting worse in Syria and fast. When the U.S. Embassy closes or "suspends operations," it sends a signal to the world that peace is off the table.

I thought about the work my colleagues and I had been doing for months. Was it all worthless? There would be no peaceful exchange of power. It was all just a pipe dream. How could we have believed and hoped for a peaceful change when violence was the most likely outcome? I had failed. I was a failure.

Additionally, the thousands of Syrians who had risked their

lives demanding reforms and a peaceful change had also failed. Peaceful protestors who had been shot, tortured, jailed, fled, vanished, and lost everything had failed.

When I arrived in Syria, I thought representing America was about fancy parties and formal meetings, but I realized that part of diplomacy was all fluff. The most important work of representing the United States occurred when Syrians took considerable risks to ask me for help. I represented the beacon of liberty that an oppressive government darkened. When I sat in back rooms whispering over coffees to someone who desired freedom, respect, and the rule of law from their own government, I found myself representing the best of America.

But there at my desk, I did not feel like a beacon. I represented the most powerful nation on earth, but in Syria we were powerless. The beacon was dimming.

There was one thing I knew I could not fail at. I needed to say goodbye to Amal. She would not take a plane to Europe in a few days and be safe with her family in another country. She was going to be in Syria when the violence came. I thought about my other Syrian friends too, how the waves of violence would also wash over them as well.

How could I leave without saying goodbye to all of them? More importantly, how could I leave without telling Amal I loved her?

I called Amal my Habibiti, my love, but had not looked her in the eyes and said the words in English, "I love you." Now I was going to leave Syria, never to return. Could I say, "I love you," and not tell her I was leaving? Would that be an asshole move?

I sat at my desk for a long time after getting the news of my permanent departure. Finally, I walked outside and smoked a few cigarettes. I tried to blow away the smoke of emotions. I needed to think logically about what to do before leaving Damascus.

As I smoked, I tried to avoid thinking about Amal and the fate of Syria. I tried to think about tangible things I could do. I had a few things in Damascus, including a car. If I tried to sell the car, questions would be raised.

It might sound strange, but I am one of those people who get attached to their cars. I have named every car I've ever had because I get so close to them. Each car drives differently and acts differently depending on the weather. They each have a personality. Spending time driving around together is one of my greatest pleasures. Having to leave my "black beauty," the name I gave to my old black Jetta, was also sad for me.

Usually, I made sure when I sold my car that it had an excellent new owner. Someone who would treat it with love and care. I have sold cars at steep discounts before to ensure the new owner is someone I want to be with my old friend. But Black Beauty would be left in Syria.

By the end of my fifth cigarette that morning, I forgot about the material things I had in Damascus. They would be lost to Syria, and there was no reason to stress about it.

I just needed to pack two suitcases with clothes and forget the rest. Maybe my things would make it out of Syria and meet me somewhere else in the world. Crazier things had happened.

Eventually, I finished my pack of cigarettes and walked back to my office. The rest of the workday dragged on as I started to clean out my desk and shred paper. I had come to terms with leaving, but I had not come to terms with not saying goodbye. I would see Amal after work and did not know how I could keep this secret from her.

After work, I drove home and awaited Amal's arrival. The minute she walked in the door and looked at me she knew something was not right. She immediately asked, "Is everything okay?"

My sadness and stress were evident on my face. I looked at her and said, "Everything is fine," adding, "just a long day at work." We went out for drinks and dinner, and we both tried to forget about the world around us.

My heart was breaking. It was most likely one of the last times I would see Amal. So, I decided I could not be sad. I pretended things were not heading toward disaster for Syria and our relationship. Instead, we enjoyed a fantastic night together.

At the end of the evening, as we said goodbye with a kiss, I knew at that moment I could not leave Syria without telling her I was leaving.

Later, alone in my dark bedroom, I wondered about our relationship. Would it or could it be a long-term love, or was this a passionate kind of love that grew out of an emotionally turbulent time in our lives? Would we ever have the chance to find out if it could work once I left Syria?

I had a terrible night's sleep, and when I did get up the next day, I decided to talk to my bosses about being allowed to tell Amal I was leaving. I did not have to tell her I thought the Embassy might be closing. I did not need to tell her violence and civil war were coming to Damascus. I just needed to tell her I was not coming back.

So, when I got to the Embassy in the morning, I went to talk to Clayton. I told her I needed to tell one person, my girlfriend, that I was leaving and not coming back. She must have seen by the look on my face and heard the tone of my voice and knew I was serious. Clayton shook her head to indicate she understood and agreed. With her support, I talked to Ford, and it was decided that I could tell Amal I was not coming back.

Getting permission to tell Amal made me very happy and extremely miserable. I would not have to fly off into the night and just leave her. But I had to face her and break her heart by saying I had to leave her.

She had told me so many times that she was grateful to find me and did not know what she would do without me. We had both become each other's greatest supporters. We had become each other's best friends. We had become intertwined through tears of happiness and sadness.

CHAPTER 32

Saying Goodbye

IT WAS THE DAY BEFORE MY DEPARTURE, and the whole day at work I could not think about the words I was writing in the sitrep. I am sure Clayton yelled at me that day for grammatical errors, but my mind was solely on what words I needed to say after work when Amal came over to my apartment.

The minute I finished the sitrep, I left work to pack and move things around my apartment. I put my clothes into two suitcases and went around the apartment collecting everything else. I grabbed everything and started making a pile in the middle of the room. The pile grew, and I was shocked at the number of things I had collected since arriving in Syria. I figured I would never see any of it again, but management had said maybe they could get it packed up later and shipped out.

It did not take long to make a pile of my possessions, so I had time to shower before Amal arrived. After showering, I sat outside on my balcony looking out at the city as the sun started to go down, but I could not find joy in the sunset.

Amal showed up at my house smiling. A huge, beautiful

smile directed right at me. When I opened my front door I picked her up and hugged and kissed her. If only we could meet every day after work like this. Smiles, laughter, and a long embrace. Why was the world tearing itself apart and ripping Amal and me away from one another?

After coming into my apartment, Amal could tell something was not normal. She was still smiling and laughing, but as she entered the living room her laughter stopped. I think the big pile of stuff in the middle of the living room might have given something away. She looked at me, then at the pile, then back at me.

"What is going on?" Amal asked.

I looked away and avoided her eyes when she asked me this question. I wanted to lie and say nothing was going on—that the pile was just in case I could not come back from vacation. But I needed and wanted to tell her the truth.

I looked into her eyes and said it: "I am not coming back from this vacation."

Tears started to roll down her face. All I could do was grab her and pull her close. As I pulled her close she cried out, and I also started to cry. We stood together sobbing in the living room next to the pile of all my meaningless belongings.

I don't know how long we stood there, and I am not sure if the Syrian security agents were crying with us as they listened.

After we pulled away from one another, wiping our faces to remove the tears, I took her hand, and we walked out on the balcony. We both lit cigarettes and started to talk.

The initial shock of the news had worn off, and now we were both trying to figure out what to say next. She never asked me why I had to leave. All she said was, "Things are going to get worse."

I was Amal's escape from reality, and she was my escape from the same reality. Now she was losing her escape, and the reality of a civil war, violence, economic collapse, and chaos came down on both of us.

As we sat there, she got more and more upset. "Why is this all happening?" she said. Her question wasn't why I was leaving, it was more than that: "Why is the whole uprising and war happening? Why could we not have met in normal times? Why could we not have spent years getting to know one another? Why is there war? Why is my country being torn apart?"

I think Amal, like many Syrians, wished the whole Arab Spring had never happened. I think they no longer wanted an uprising. The cost was too much. Their lives were okay before the Arab Spring. It was not perfect, they lacked many freedoms, but it was stable and safe. It was possible to have hope and life.

At that moment on the balcony, I was truly disgusted with the Syrian uprising. I hated all of it. I hated the hope it had brought to thousands of Syrians who took to the streets to demand their human rights. I hated the regime for resorting to violence to stop them. I hated the opposition for not being able to force the regime into reforms. I hated Syrian security forces, and I hated peaceful protestors. I hated our U.S. policy on Syria and our policymakers. I hated all of them, everything and everyone.

The only good thing that night was my love for Amal. I was unsure before the night if I would tell her, but now I knew I could.

After looking out at Syria burn red with the setting sun, we walked inside. We laid down on my bed and got so close to one another that our eyes were staring into the other one's soul. We got to that level of closeness only two people in love can reach. It was at that moment that I whispered the words into her ear. I said, "I love you."

She pulled back from me slightly, and now I could see her entire face. She smiled at me and responded, "I also love you."

Those words meant we were not giving up. This night might not be our last night together. Maybe we could still be together even though we would be far apart.

We could not plan our futures. I had no idea where I was going, and Amal had no idea what would happen in Syria. We were both lost, but maybe we could find each other someday in the future.

Eventually, we got out of bed and went back to the balcony. Standing there in the cool night air, we gazed out at so many unknowns. That night we never said, "Don't worry, things will be okay." We could not sugarcoat reality and escape into drinks and laughter. It seemed like all we could do was hold one another and not speak. Neither of us wanted to tell the other person a lie.

Well after midnight, it was time for Amal to head home. We cried and embraced at the door. As she turned and walked away, I slowly closed the door to my apartment. Again, I cried in my bed alone.

CHAPTER 33

Going Away

WHEN I OPENED MY EYES THE NEXT MORNING, the first thing I did was message Amal. I wrote, "I hope you did not cry too much last night."

I wanted to be a person in her life who only gave pleasure and joy, but instead, I was causing her pain. At the same time, I did not care if it was painful.

I begged her to come over one more time before I left. I wrote to her, "Please come over. Spend a few hours with me."

Her response popped up on my phone a few seconds later and I was nervous to even read it. She said, "I don't know. I really don't know. I am very very sad at heart."

I responded by saying, "Please just come and see me for an hour or just come and let me give you a hug."

Amal responded by sending me the name of a song. She sent me the name of the Pink Floyd song "Time HQ." I pulled out my laptop and looked up the song.

While listening, one line stood out to me: "The time is gone, the song is over, thought I'd something more to say." After she sent me the name of the song I did not receive any more messages from her that morning. Maybe the night before had been our last time together.

On my way to my last day of work, the song kept playing in my head. That one line on repeat. Once I got to the Embassy, I packed up my final office trinkets, got the sitrep done, and put on my Out of Office, which just noted I had gone on vacation.

I said my goodbyes to my colleagues. Saying goodbye to all of them was easy. I knew they had the ability to leave Syria. I knew that they were all there by choice, but still hoped they got out before the regime decided to do anything to them.

I wished my bosses the best of luck and left the Embassy at the end of the day in my black leather Shabiha jacket. I was jealous of them because I wanted to stay with them until the end. Could I just say that I was not going on R&R and stay? The answer was no. I had to leave.

As I drove home for the last time, I still did not know if Amal would come over to say goodbye. The last thing she had messaged me that afternoon was, "This is the worst day in years... I cannot work. I feel sick in my stomach."

When I got home, I found a few more things to add to the pile in the middle of the room. I felt like an empty shell wandering around my empty apartment.

The night before, I had felt something different in that same location. Amal had greeted me with such a smile when she came to the door. I was over the moon when we both said we loved each other. I was sad I was leaving, but I also felt love. Now I felt nothing. I was empty.

Then, suddenly, there was a buzz at my door. When I opened it, there she stood. She was a mess. Her eyes were red, and her lips were quivering. We rushed into each other's arms, and as we kissed, I could taste the salt from her tears.

I really cannot remember how long we stayed together that last night. It could have been two minutes; it could have been an hour. Either way, it was too short. I wanted Damascus, Syria, the Middle East, the entire world to go away. I wanted to be left alone with her forever, just the two of us. Instead, Amal came just to say goodbye. She never ventured farther than the front hallway of my apartment that night.

She left as she arrived, sad and full of tears. "I love you," she said, and I responded, "I love you too." With that, she walked out the door. She was gone into the night, and I was alone, sobbing in an empty apartment.

CHAPTER 34

Tragic Love

THE NEXT TWELVE HOURS WERE A BLUR. I went back to the balcony for a few more smokes until I got the call that an Embassy driver was downstairs, ready to take me to the airport. I placed my bags next to the elevator and returned to the apartment for the final time.

I stood next to the pile on the living room floor, which now reached about one meter in height. On the very top of the pile, I placed the keys to Black Beauty. With that, I turned and walked out.

A few diplomats from other countries were on my flight out, but I was in no mood or condition to make small talk. I tried to sleep, but it was impossible. I arrived after a few connections very early the following day at Schiphol airport in Holland. My parents were there waiting for me with open arms. They asked me why I had so many bags for a two-week vacation. I just said I was not returning to Damascus. They tried to ask me more questions, but I could not answer any of them that first day.

Later in the morning, away from my family, I opened my

laptop to find a message from Amal. It said, "I love you too, Shawn. You are one of the nicest things that have ever happened to me."

Sitting with a cup of hot coffee, I realized I was a world away from Syria. A few hours on an airplane transported my physical body to a completely different world. But my mind was still in Damascus, and my heart still ached for the one who lived there.

I listened to a song she sent me, "Dreaming Light" by Anathema. The words in the song echoed my feelings: "I feel you, but I don't know you. I dreamed of you from the moment I saw you. And I've seen the sunrise in your eyes. The sky, the sea, the light."

Now we could only dream about being in the same place. Dream of a Syria without violence. Dream of a world where we could travel, live, and be together. Dream of a love that would not be killed or destroyed by an uprising or an evil regime. No one could stop us from daydreaming. Nothing could stop us from being in different places and making up our dream life together.

However, on December 23, our dreams turned into nightmares. Amal messaged me that morning and said, "Explosions in Damascus. I woke up to the sounds. I guess violence has finally reached Damascus."

This message, this moment in time, marked the end of our love story during a revolution. The uprising was over. The Syrian Civil War had begun.

It did not, however, mark the end of our story. Just like Syria, our love story was tragic. But that story is for another time.

Made in United States
North Haven, CT
31 March 2023

34860367R00124